Praise for Designed for Learning

"*Designed for Learning* is a thrilling and timely clarion call to modern educational systems to resurrect morality and transference of wisdom as the core of a learner-centered instructional model. Wimberley artfully evaluates the modern trends of digital environments, the substantial ramifications of social media, and the compelling potential these trends have on education in the digital age. He unabashedly indicts humanistic and relativistic amoral and moral-neutral promotion of the self in modern education while expertly defining the characteristics of a shepherd heart teacher who imparts wisdom to students, leads from a moral center, and facilitates discerning mastery learning in a digital age where information, destructive and constructive, is ubiquitous. This book is a must-read for the educator and educational leader who yearns for challenges to the status quo and craves abundant opportunities for their students."
—**Nathan Street**, EdD, director of Fine Arts, Guilford County Schools, Greensboro, North Carolina

"*Designed for Learning* is a much-needed look into how we can successfully lead our newest generation of students who are growing up digital. Wimberley understands the serious consequences of a generation of students with no true north on their moral compass due to the influence of the internet and a constant connection to information that may not be emotionally appropriate for them. Online opportunities have changed the way students learn, but also transformed how instruction can occur. A combination of focusing on moral values with various forms of instructional techniques may just help create a generation of connected, compassionate members of society who can take charge and lead in the future."
—**Benji Morrell**, assistant principal, Cobb County School District, Marietta, GA

"*Designed for Learning* is a must-read for veteran and new teachers alike. With the educational community and society embracing advances in technology and its inclusion in learning environments, what is often forgotten is both what a teacher brings to their students as well as a true plan for how to best utilize both the strengths of the technology and the educator. This book does a splendid job of allowing the reader to take a step back and realize that not only is the educator paramount to the development of students but it is possible to reap the benefits of technology and not lose the valuable contributions our professional educators make toward the growth of our young learners. It gives an honest and practical reminder that education goes beyond standards and that technology cannot replace what a passionate educator can bring to their students."

—**Kevin Popadines**, EdD

"In a day when personalized learning systems and blended learning platforms are being implemented into the educational process, *Designed for Learning* is a reminder of the vital role of a quality teacher in successful educational transformation. Wimberley adds, 'It's not a matter of replacing teachers with technology. It's a matter of leveraging technology to do what it does best . . . engaging with a kid.' As a former teacher and now adjunct professor at several educational institutions, Wimberley understands the value that next-generation, personalized learning platforms bring to today's educational landscapes, yet he reveals in many definitive statements and examples throughout the book the paramount guidance and value a quality teacher brings to this process. I wholeheartedly recommend this book for all individuals involved in education at any level."
—**Jason Haas**, EdD, director of Programs and Services, NCCSA (North Carolina Christian School Association)

"Dr. Wimberley's passion for education resonates throughout the pages of *Designed for Learning* as he draws from decades of education experience and offers sage wisdom on what it takes to motivate today's student. This book toggles between theory and practice and confirms what research and educators have long believed—creating relationships with students that enhances their self-worth is critically important as educators prepare students for the complex world they are inheriting. Channeling the powerful imagery of shepherding, Wimberley systemically guides the reader through practical steps for engaging today's digital-centric student. Schooling as we have previously known it has changed at an unprecedented pace; this said, every leader looking to transform learning environments to meet the needs of our complex world need to read this book."
—**Terry W. Burwell**, EdD, principal, Ontario, Canada

"Wimberley has penned true words of wisdom that reach out and minister to those educators with a shepard's heart. He provides them with a clear and concise roadmap to bring a strong moral code into the classroom without involving religion or politics while building a solid educational foundation within the country's future leaders. By incorporating classic

curriculum into the digital era of pedagogy, he is equipping shepherds to empower and inspire students into a lifelong love affair of learning. This book is for those with a heart-felt desire to see what is good and virtuous borne in classrooms and spread to world for the benefit of everyone."
—**Lane Melton**, MEd

"As a twenty-five-plus year veteran of the classroom—finding success at the secondary, undergraduate, and graduate level—I have become keenly aware that today's educational model is not in the best interest of our students—our teachers—our future. In *Designed for Learning*, Wimberley speaks to the very heart of the pedagogical framework that will meet the needs of today's learners. I highly recommended it. Multiple times throughout the reading, the author had me wanting to jump out of my seat to shout, 'YES!' Educators at every level would benefit from the insight and understanding that Wimberley brings forth."
—**Nathan C. Hamblin**, EdD, educator, mentor, District Leadership Team; editor/consultant, Educational Researcher

DESIGNED FOR LEARNING

DESIGNED FOR LEARNING

*Transferring Wisdom
to Digital Generations*

Alan Wimberley, EdD

ROWMAN & LITTLEFIELD
Lanham • Boulder • New York • London

Published by Rowman & Littlefield
An imprint of The Rowman & Littlefield Publishing Group, Inc.
4501 Forbes Boulevard, Suite 200, Lanham, Maryland 20706
www.rowman.com

Unit A, Whitacre Mews, 26-34 Stannary Street, London SE11 4AB

Copyright © 2018 by Alan Wimberley

All rights reserved. No part of this book may be reproduced in any form or by any electronic or mechanical means, including information storage and retrieval systems, without written permission from the publisher, except by a reviewer who may quote passages in a review.

British Library Cataloguing in Publication Information Available

Library of Congress Cataloging-in-Publication Data Available

ISBN: 978-1-4758-3616-5 (cloth : alk. paper)
ISBN: 978-1-4758-3617-2 (pbk. : alk. paper)
ISBN: 978-1-4758-3618-9 (electronic)

To my wonderful wife of thirty-eight years, Bonnie Belle.

All I know about shepherding others, I learned from watching you. Though I'm grateful for all things about you, I am most thankful for your patience with me. I've watched, listened, and learned from you as you've accomplished such great things for kids and teachers.

I fervently agree with our grandchildren: "Spending the day with BB is the best day."

CONTENTS

Acknowledgments	ix
Introduction	xi
1 The Shepherd Heart Teacher	1
2 The World of Digital Generations	19
3 The Moral Education Parallel for the Shepherd Heart Teacher	35
4 The Silhouette: Belief Systems of Shepherd Heart Educators	47
5 The Distinction of Morality in Education	55
6 Points of Wisdom and the Curriculum of the Shepherd	63
7 The Academic Parallel Structure for the Shepherd Heart Teacher	77
8 The Education Theory for Transformed Learning Systems	97
9 Models of the Theory	107
10 The Anchor of Morality and Wisdom in Educating Digital Learners	113
About the Author	119

ACKNOWLEDGMENTS

No book about education can be written without a lot of counsel and help. While it might be nice to think that one can create something alone, the truth is that a lot of people, experiences, and relationships play a part of any accomplishment. Such is the case here. Though it's impossible to mention everyone, it's always important to remember particular individuals. And specifically in a book about being a shepherd heart educator, those individuals each had a significant influence on the thoughts and ideas presented here.

Bill Midkiff ("Chief") made such a difference in my life during my middle school years. He taught me a lot about important things even beyond the classroom. And he taught me to drive. Whether or not I actually ever have to use algebra every day (and I don't), I do have to drive. Thanks, Chief. You were the first teacher who invested well in my life.

My 77s, a most interesting and valuable gang of friends from my high school years, taught me so much back then and continue to teach me today. Their wisdom, counsel, and friendship are constant reminders to me that shepherd hearts aren't exclusive to classroom teachers. Whether we are texting each other just to make sure everybody's okay or just hanging out at the farm, this unique group of friends has served, throughout my life, as a center of stability and encouragement.

My doctoral candidates, both at Dallas Baptist University and Liberty University, are treasured friends and colleagues. While I've not done anything great in my life, I have had the amazing opportunity to speak into the hearts and lives of some who are doing great things. These candidates, located all over the country, give themselves each day for others. Their work is scholarly and intellectual. And their friendship is counted among the most valuable components of my life.

Dr. Neil Dugger has proven to be one who knows the heart well, encourages educators to go beyond even their own expectations, and drives home the best qualities of teaching and administration for the sake of learners. He is my friend but, most importantly, he is a friend to many affected by his leadership.

Tim Harkins, one of the most gifted men I've known, doesn't know it but his friendship and counsel provided so much inspiration and foundation for much of what readers will find here. His ability to connect with so many while making each one feel like he is their best friend, and do that in such a genuine way, has become a significant part of my life.

This book could not have happened without the editing expertise of Dr. Nathan Hamblin. Not only was he a scholarly student and doctoral candidate but his intellect and servant heart also proved valuable for this work. As always, Dr. Tom Koerner and his team at Rowman & Littlefield proved to be wonderful to work with once again.

Additionally, I am grateful for the continued friendship with Dr. Kathleen O'Toole. She is an accomplished classical educator and her assistance and counsel on the section related to classical curriculum proved to be of the highest caliber.

Lastly, I thank those who have taught me what a shepherd's heart looks like: my three sons, Isaac, Micah, and Aaron. As I've watched these men shepherd their families, I've become more aware of those areas in which I need to grow. They sharpen me and provide significant models of the shepherd heart each of us should have for those we lead and teach. Being a parent of young children in a digital world can be difficult to navigate. While I enjoyed every minute with these young fathers when they were themselves children, I find that the best moments are now, watching them shepherd their own children, my grandchildren, and naturally practice the best qualities of the shepherd.

INTRODUCTION

Education is transforming from teaching systems that focused on teacher-direct classrooms to learning systems focusing on student-centered education. As this transformation occurs and accelerates, there are already major attempts to define what the role of teachers will be. The primary function, as currently thought, will be to minimize the significance of the teacher in the classroom by relegating these professionals to facilitator positions in technology-driven education.

In my work as an education architect, as I consider the transformation, my hope is to articulate some things that have to be given priority because of the innovative and increasing waves of technology that not only push into the world of education but also push into the world at large. And in that consideration, I am reminded of a common story, told often, that underlines our best role in a classroom.

The story is of the preschooler who was afraid of the dark. He just couldn't sleep alone in his room and always ended up wanting to sleep in his parents' bed at night. As he lay there each night, he would softly whisper to his father, "Daddy, is your face turned toward me?" And his dad would softly tell him, "Yes, my face is turned toward you." And each night, the boy would fall asleep feeling safe and protected.[1]

My wife and I raised three sons. Each was different and each was the same in so many ways. As a young dad, I was busy trying to figure out how to conquer the world and make the car payment each month. And as a dad who wanted to make sure my boys knew I loved them, I always tried to make sure they received the attention that growing children need from parents.

But as attentive as I tried to be, sometimes I was so busy even when home. And when one of them would come in to show me the latest picture he had drawn or to tell me the story of his day, I would, as parents often do, give a cursory nod or "yeah, that's great, buddy." Now, it's not that I wasn't interested. But we just get busy.

Well, it always worked. Until it didn't. One of the boys figured it out at a very early age, and when he would show me that picture, he would stand there with it and watch my face and my eyes. He was waiting; giving the verbal acknowledgment wasn't good enough for him. Nodding my head while still attending to whatever task was at hand wasn't going to work with this one. He would stand there watching me, my face, and my eyes. He wanted my attention, not just my words and nods. He needed to know that I was engaged.

He needed to know my attention and encouragement was genuine. Only when I dropped what I was doing, stopped what I was doing, and focused my full attention on the drawing would he be satisfied. Only when I commented on something that proved I was actually paying attention would he be happy and move on to his next adventure.

Can we, should we, will we replace teachers with technology? This always seems to be where every argument goes. I have opportunities to teach graduate students in education administration and when the subject turns to twenty-first-century innovation, the debate always turns to replacing teachers with technology. That seems to be the great notion. So can we, should we, will we?

Motivation is a key to learning. If a kid sits in the classroom and has no motivation, extrinsic or intrinsic, it really doesn't matter what we do. The kid won't learn.

Engagement is a key to learning. Buy the books, line them up in rows, make them sit up and pay attention. But if they don't engage, they won't learn.

They may show up and they may even "pass" our class. That doesn't mean they've learned.

We have gone too far in our definition of "teaching" and made it something it isn't meant to be. We've morphed the idea of teaching into something akin to university professorships that start at the top of the heap with Ivy League "old-school" lecturers and then scale down to the high school (and even elementary school) levels. This, and only (or mostly) this, is teaching.

Subject matter experts that prepare their presentations and deliver them each day to enraptured students: that's the pure idea and "teaching" wherever we are tries to get as close to that as possible. If we do that, we have done our job. That's the visual we get when "teaching" is mentioned.

Thinking about engagement, one typically arrives at the conclusion that we need to find ways to engage the student with the content or material needing to be learned. Yet in an Industrial Age system of education in which the job of "teaching" was accomplished by performing the tasks of "teaching" as defined by that system, engagement may or may not have occurred.

I've been a subject matter expert and I've taught. I've worked in plenty of situations in which the job of teaching can be done. And I have found myself on the slippery slope of giving cursory nods with a hearty "that's great, buddy" to kids. It's too easy to care more about my subject than my students (or at least all my students). It's too easy to get caught up in the administrative and the busyness of the job and never have the time for the kids or the kid.

If it's defined as the pure idea of lecturer and subject-driven interaction, it's easy. What's hard is engagement. True engagement for each student.

No computer ever motivated me to do more and be more. No software program ever inspired me to stretch myself intellectually.

I think we've picked on the kid somewhat excessively in the engagement debate. They don't care. They don't apply themselves. They don't engage with the learning process.

We often just have disengaged teachers. Technology cannot replace teachers because an engaged adult passing knowledge and wisdom to younger generations has always been a hallmark of successful learning. But (and hopefully we can help with this) what kind of engagement? It's not as simple as one might think.

It's not a matter of replacing teachers with technology. It's a matter of leveraging technology to do what it does best. So a teacher can do what he or she should do best: engage with a kid, to motivate, to encourage, and to be the change and growth agent for that child. That's legacy living. We have the opportunity to do it now more than ever.

A teacher, when faced with the burdens of too many students, just couldn't get to it all. Now, they can. And we should create the systems where they have that opportunity. We shouldn't replace them. We should free them up. Only then can every kid know that "yes, my face is turned toward you."

This book will articulate the tremendous opportunity we now have to leverage the incredible talents, skills, and gifts of teachers to optimize transformed learning environments. The concept of conscientious engagement, purposeful and passionate, will be introduced and articulated. The book will focus on the major components of classical curriculum and moral education that has composed traditional content for centuries and how that can be strengthened through the engagement of what we call "shepherd heart teachers."

Shepherd heart teachers know who they are. While the book doesn't exclude or judge anyone, it will most connect with those who see themselves in that passionate role: to shepherd students as never before because the digital world is changing and will one day have no semblance to the world we've known or even the one we know now. It cannot be stressed enough that this book speaks to a particular type of teacher while admitting that not every teacher may define themselves thusly. And the book makes no statement that the teacher as defined here is the best teacher, the only teacher that helps kids. But the idea of the shepherd heart is crucial.

We cannot afford to possibly disenfranchise educators with a wrong definition or perception of "facilitating." As we transform education, this foundation of knowledge will be even more important to give students the best opportunities, ensure reliable and effective leadership as these generations of learners move to their future place in society, and encourage today's teacher to step into a greater role in the classroom rather than stepping off to the side.

Each generation of learners must learn a body of information and convert that to knowledge that ensures success and efficacy. Even more important, though, is the transfer of wisdom and morality from generation to generation. That demands a solid and stable educator workforce that is passionate and purposeful, taking advantage of the opportunity to engage in an effective manner. That transfer of wisdom and morality is significant.

INTRODUCTION

This book serves as a challenge to educators to no longer give allegiance to an outdated conventional teaching system, refuse to be pushed aside, and understand the new role to focus on wisdom and shepherding in classrooms in transformed learning systems.

I was raised in a small town in north central Texas. It was the greatest little town complete with everything one would think about growing up in a small town in the mid-part of the past century. I still go back there to visit at times. And it hasn't changed much, thank goodness. It still remains a great place to grow up.

I remember being excused from high school classes when large grass fires broke out and threatened to spread their damage across acres of property. I remember that old water tower, a challenge to every adolescent kid who had something to say for the world to see and loaded with enough courage and spray paint to say it. I remember the best teachers, the best friends, and the best years.

My dad owned the only gas station in town. And I spent most of my days pumping gas, changing oil, and fixing flat tires. It was good work and it taught me a lot. Nobody cleans a windshield better than I do.

Back then, emergency services were all volunteer. We had great emergency vehicles, fire trucks, and an ambulance that were all manned by volunteers in town who would get to those vehicles and get to a scene to put out fires or rescue victims. As teenagers, we would drive around at night just hanging out in a quiet town that had no open businesses, no traffic lights, and no law enforcement. But if we heard that siren go off, we would stop whatever important things we were doing and rush to help.

This was before 911 existed. Our alarm system was very efficient though. Throughout town, certain phones were rigged to ring continuously should someone call the local emergency number. The ring would continue without pause until someone would answer. These phones sat in the homes or businesses where the volunteers were most likely to be during the day or evening. That system did the job for an all-volunteer force.

One of these phones sat on the counter at my dad's service station. Now, my dad had an old gas stove under the window with several metal lawn chairs in a semicircle that served as a hangout place for customers or old men on their rounds every day. Most likely, someone on that volunteer force would be within hearing distance of that phone should there be a vehicle accident out on the highway or a burning house in desperate need of water.

And on plenty of occasions, I'd be one of those who answered that call and race to the scene. I got to help those heroes who still serve people in that small town even today. Small towns tend to grow heroes like that.

Often, rather than racing to the shelter where the emergency vehicles were housed and getting to a scene in the fire truck or ambulance, I would head to my car and get to a scene, being one of the first to arrive. I remember this occurring a few times, when I arrived first, assessed an accident, and could actually give the guys the most important information about victims and the most urgent needs upon their arrival. It's called triage and I was honored as a kid to just do my part. That triage could help them know what needed to be done first and who needed emergency care the most when they arrived.

I remember one particular incident in which we were at a scene of an accident and the men were giving immediate and urgent care to a victim who needed it badly. There were several people involved but this one definitely needed attention right then. I noticed, though, that other cars had stopped on the highway and some people had gotten out to walk to the scene—not to help but to watch. This happens at scenes.

The problem is when watchers start trying to direct or redirect the responders. In small towns with limited resources, and certainly back in the 1970s, that's pretty common. But on this occasion, someone watching began urging the men to stop working on that victim and direct their attention to another person.

And when they ignored the person, he became more insistent. But they just continued doing their work. The person attempting to redirect their attention wasn't helping. He didn't understand the urgency but that didn't stop him from walking up and giving orders. In the end, it all paid off. All survived.

Teachers can often feel like they are doing triage, trying to assess who needs the most help and needs it urgently. We may feel that we are sometimes just putting Band-Aids on wounds and splints on broken limbs of learning in our classrooms. And it doesn't help when those who don't do what we do walk on the scene and interject strong opinions and unsolicited commands to stop what we are doing and do something else.

I've personally been told to "forget" about some kids because they just didn't have the capacity to succeed. Teachers live with an incredible responsibility on their shoulders and in their minds every day. Their calling in this life is great because we depend on their ability to give our next generations what they need to survive, thrive, and lead in the future. Yet we sometimes can become nothing more than a passerby who walks on the scene of the accident and starts pointing fingers, assigning blame, and barking orders.

So let me start by saying that I was never a hometown hero when I had the privilege of helping those hometown heroes of my youth. And I have never been the rock-star teacher who just seemed to know what to do every time for every kid. However, and this is important, I'm also not that passerby who just walks in thinking I know better and everything I say is truth.

In my work with educators, I am first and foremost a teacher. And just as I was proud of being among those volunteers so many years ago in that small town, I am proud to be counted among a body of incredible life-changing educators who give themselves for kids every day. What we do is important.

Now, even as I might caution us about the passerby who might be seen as someone to ignore, I am also quick to point out that we have to be humble in what we do. We truly don't have all the answers. Anyone who might tell you that just hasn't been presented with enough questions yet. Why? Because working with students is humbling and it teaches you that you don't have all the answers. So maybe, instead of ignoring any counsel from any passerby, we should listen sometimes.

When I am working with educators, one of the best paradigms I can have is to remember that I am teaching *learners* rather than teaching *teachers*. We can't stop learning. We can often believe that, once we have achieved the degree and are now teaching, there's nothing left to learn beyond the occasional professional development. We just need to sharpen up what we already know. But that limits our ability to actually learn and grow.

The passerby can be hard to take sometimes because if you are a true teacher with a passion to help kids, you just have a different approach to even the most common things. But that doesn't mean we should always ignore it. The best teachers are also the best learners because we also have such a heightened sensitivity toward kids.

Not long ago, I was watching television on a Saturday afternoon when I should have been mowing the lawn. I was scanning the channels and ended up watching a few moments of a baseball game. I usually don't watch baseball on television, but something caught my eye. The batter had just hit a long fly ball that was surely a home run. However, just before the ball sailed over the wall into the stands, the fielder leaped and caught it on the fly. What a catch! The home team crowd went wild.

As the camera stayed on the fielder, an interesting scene unfolded. There were two boys in the stands, both with gloves. The stands were mostly empty in that area except for these two young fans. The fielder walked toward the boys, who were both holding out their gloves, wanting that prize ball. One was in the first row; the other in the second row.

As the fielder got closer, both boys held out those gloves, waiting for him to pitch the ball to them. He walked right up to the stands within inches of the boy in the first row. He then motioned to the boy in the second row, who hurriedly ran to the railing. The fielder dropped the ball into the boy's glove. He then turned back to his position on the field.

The boy with the ball held it high as he walked back to his seat directly behind the first boy. The announcers seized on the opportunity to laud the player for his gracious act. The camera stayed on the scene while the announcers talked about the boy's prize and the player's gift. As I watched, though, my attention was drawn to the first boy, the one who was passed over. Because both boys were sitting in the same area and the player on the field was also in the same general location, all three were in the camera shot.

The cameraman wanted to get shots of the second boy (the one with the ball) and the player during the announcers' comments. In fact, the camera shot back to the scene two more times before the commercial break. The problem was that each time the camera zoomed in, the first boy was also there. And while the producers of the broadcast wanted the viewer to focus on the second boy and the player, my attention was solely drawn to the first boy.

It was obvious the boy was disappointed. But as the scene continued, his disappointment turned to embarrassment. Finally, by the third shot, the boy slowly covered his face with his empty glove, hiding his tears from a national audience. As I watched, my heart broke for the kid. I don't think it was the fact that he didn't have the ball that hurt the most. I don't think it was the fact that someone else was chosen over him that hurt the most.

INTRODUCTION   xix

What hurt the most was that his being *unchosen* was being broadcast for everyone to see. The camera, so focused on the chosen kid with the ball and the terrific fielder who had made the kid's day, was also letting everyone have a view of the first kid's disappointment, sadness, and embarrassment.

That glove, brought to the game to hold a baseball, instead was used to hide his face from all of us. One kid was going home with a ball in his glove and a story he would tell for the rest of his life. The other would go home with an empty glove and a memory that would hurt every time he thought of it.

As I watched, I got mad. Not at the player. How could I fault him? He didn't do anything wrong. I couldn't fault the second kid who received the ball. He was just being a kid. I was mad because I wanted both boys to have a ball.

In fact, I thought the perfect ending to the story would be for someone at the game to go to the concession stand, buy a ball, find that boy, and give it to him. Or maybe the player could have asked for a second ball and trotted over to the kid later. Either way, my one thought was this: *give 'em both a ball.*

We have somewhat the same situation in our education systems. It is a truth that, no matter how much we trumpeted our success in the old teaching systems, students were being left behind. The traditional mode of teaching in the past was based on a timed system that demands students keep up, stay with the pack, and learn it at the same pace as the brightest kids. If you can't meet that demand, you get left behind. Too many kids left with empty gloves.

Here's the saddest part: while we're so busy focusing on the successful kids, the spotlight also shines on those who aren't going to make it. No wonder so many of them drop out. It could just be their way of covering their face with the empty glove. And even those students who do well get frustrated with conventional teaching systems in which the teacher is the star.

While we haven't arrived with a broad, full-scale transformed educational environment yet, we are getting closer every year. What's seen as new and innovative is now becoming standard for some and will one day become our mode of education broadly. We are transforming.

Teachers have a broken heart for every kid. They think differently. They want every kid to have a ball in that glove. However, and this is the reason for this book, while we are standing on the brink of being able to transform everything, we might make some mistakes in doing so if we are not careful to have some understandings about the role of a teacher in the emerging learning systems.

We will address the two most important roles in the book. Hopefully, it can help us define better what a *facilitator* is and how this will be the key for learning systems engagement. And just as importantly, we can help define the need for teachers to be *attainable and relevant moral exemplars*[2] in the classroom. Not only is education changing but the elements of moral education, presented through research for the past thirty years or so, also need a place in our schools.

The rise of a digitally controlled world makes this generation of learners different than previous generations. Our teachers, acting in the role of accurately defined facilitators and narrowly defined relevant moral exemplars, can raise their significance in the digital learning systems environment. Generations of learners will benefit from these teachers even more than they did when the teacher was a lecturing controller of all information.

We must not separate the two most important things we have to do for digital generations. And we can view these as parallels. *These are the academic parallel and the moral education parallel.* We must have both. In the digital environment, these students are different simply because the world has changed. Yet for them this world hasn't changed. They have had this world from the beginning.

There is a great need to address the academic benefits of transformed learning systems. And defining what facilitation is now, rather than what we thought it was, is crucial for us. It's not what we were told when we went to college. Hopefully, we can frame something here that can help us.

But there is also a need to address the significance of engaging with students in a way that helps them develop a greater moral reasoning. The digital world loves itself and pushes the self on kids every day. We must be engaged with these learners to help them understand the elements of morality and wisdom. Again, hopefully, this can help.

In this book, we will look at a particular kind of teacher. As I said, no one speaks for everybody and no one has all the answers. I certainly hold no thought that I am somehow the spokesman for every piece or person in education. This book is particularly for those educators who find themselves fitting within the profiles outlined in these chapters. However, that profile is significant for these digital generations.

This isn't a book about any particular type of educational plan or pursuit that becomes the end-all answer for every learner. It's not about charter schools being the answer. Nor is it about the local district being the answer. It's not an advocate for private schools or homeschooling. It's just about the adult who closes the door and gives him- or herself every day to help kids.

It's also not about any particular type of student population. We have learners coming from rural, urban, and suburban environments. We have learners who live in the most difficult situations. And we have learners coming from comfortable homes. We have so many students with so many different backgrounds. No matter the living conditions, the demographics, or the opportunities or lack of opportunities, each deserves our best.

This book is about all of us, no matter our background and preparation, giving everything we have for these generations of learners. We should not disqualify any adult, one who has proven his or her passion and willingness to spend his or her life to pour into kids, from helping kids. While we know that there may be particular differences in our schools, populations, choices, and opportunities, can we focus on transferring wisdom, morality, and solid learning opportunities to this generation?

We can if we don't use anything related to this to champion our own particular choices and preferences. We can as long as we first get along as adults and remember that we are all just trying to help.

For years, we have been talking about teaching to the *whole child*. That's a good concept and a worthy pursuit in the classroom. However, this book, hopefully, leads us to consider teaching to the *whole teacher*. If we can undefine some things that the old systems wrongly defined for us and redefine how these things are in transformed learning systems, we will reach the *whole teacher*.

Teaching to the *whole teacher* means that we train, expect, and support the teacher to be more than just a practitioner in the classroom. If we have the most passionate and most caring adult in that room with our children, we want that adult to be doing more than teaching academic skills and information. We want that person to be engaged in an intentional way, investing him- or herself in a way that changes lives.

We don't want our children to be patted on the head and receive empty praise just to make them feel good about themselves. We need a wise, moral adult pouring themselves into those children, speaking into their lives and giving them so much more. We want them to change lives.

Teaching to the *whole teacher* offers much more than professional development that focuses only on the practitioner.

Digital learners deserve our best. At no time in our history have we had the opportunity to give them that more than now. Read on and let's see what we can do.

NOTES

1. A. Wimberley, "Yes, My Face Is Turned Toward You," blog post, June 2, 2014, http://alanwimberley.com/yes-my-face-is-turned-toward-you/.

2. H. Han, J. Kim, C. Jeong, and G. Cohen, "Attainable and Relevant Moral Exemplars Are More Effective Than Extraordinary Exemplars in Promoting Voluntary Service Engagement," *Frontiers in Psychology* 8 (2017), doi:10.3389/fpsyg.2017.00283.

1

THE SHEPHERD HEART TEACHER

> Educating the mind without educating the heart is no education at all.
> —Aristotle

If you ask the average person to name one individual who made the greatest positive difference in his or her life, most often than not, the response would be a teacher. We spend such an inordinate amount of time, in our younger years, with those adults who teach us, mentor us, and guide us along the way. And that time is intentionally significant because we are learning, changing our ideas, and formulating what we know and believe about our world.

It could be a homeschool kitchen. It could be a classroom. It could be a football field. As we are growing up, we are constantly being watched. We are cautioned, warned, encouraged, and discouraged by adults. We are taught.

No one learns in a vacuum. Something or someone is always teaching us. And those young years are significant. We imprint on people and things in ways that stick with us long after we have to have jobs just to make a mortgage. Those who teach us fill up the files in our head for a lifetime. We may be grateful for some. We may be hurt by some. But we are certainly affected by most.

But somewhere in those files is that teacher, that adult who showed an uncommon love for us and who made the difference and made us feel we were okay. So many can state that they are who they are because of a teacher, for better or worse. It's pretty heady stuff to be a teacher.

Teaching is a sacred calling. In our day of rules and regulations, policies and practice, we cannot forget that teaching is a sacred calling. Too often, we've suffered from the professional educator: those who see it as a good gig; show up, fill out the paperwork, open the book, and let's follow along together.

Professional educators may not see the neurological wiring they're responsible for in that child. They say things, do things, and believe things about children that can be uncaring and hurtful. And hurtful can become harmful without the intervention of the advocate for that child. Countless numbers among us have probably been more affected, even motivated, by the hurtful and harmful interactions with an uncaring professional educator. There is no sacredness in what they do.

But that's not the typical story. Most teachers are passionate, sacred people when it comes to what they do and why they do it. These adults (and they deserve their paychecks) don't do what they do for a paycheck. These adults (and they deserve to be encouraged) do this even when it's discouraging. Not to be too dramatic, but a teacher does lose sleep sometimes because of that kid. On the scales in this life, we need those teachers to far outweigh those who shouldn't be doing this. And they do. The sacred effects of a teacher on us cannot be ignored.

So for the purposes of this book, we will leave the lesson plans behind. We will not be focusing on best practice, lunch duty, or professional development. We will be taking the "job" out of the job. If there's any hope in this book, it's that we can step back and remember why we are doing this. It's a calling.

The teachers specifically addressed in this book are shepherds. While one might believe this includes anyone and everyone engaged with education, that's not necessarily the purpose. This book will be geared to that individual who changes lives specifically in the realms pointed out here. While one might not agree with everything written, the purpose is to define those educators in a particular way. These are "shepherd heart teachers."

This will be emphasized often. It's not a cheerleading manual written to make one feel good. It's not a motivational book that hopes to inspire anyone. It's not meant to excuse bad teachers and uncaring adults. It's not written to indict or ignite anyone. There's no blind eye or deaf ear to the problems we have in education. But there is a definitive purpose in this book. You won't agree with everything here because, to meet the demands of writing this, it will be required to be intentional about a lot of things.

The premise is that these kinds of teachers are shepherds. And if they're shepherds, what does that mean and what should we be doing? You may realize, rightly so, that so much of the "personal" is in here. It comes from a lifetime of being in and around educators and education, watching generations of learners graduate each year: a subject matter expert with a lot of caution about the subject matter.

As each generation has moved on, there is a significant feeling of responsibility. We can do all the professional development we want, make all the laws we want, and create the new ways to do the old things all day long. But something is going on here.

And we have to be intentional in the definition of a shepherd heart teacher. Some won't fit that definition. This isn't to say that anyone not fitting that description is any less, or more, of a teacher. It just means they may not fit the description of a shepherd heart teacher as defined here.

We are not debating the merits of anyone. We are merely pulling out a specific identification for educators who engage with digital generations and affixing a defined, concise term: *the shepherd heart teacher.*

Each year, an entire population of students stops and smiles for a camera, diploma in hand. They look so grown up. And they move on. They fail, they succeed, they marry, and they have kids. They make mistakes and they make their own way. They become us. Hopefully, they'll look after us when we are done.

As each layer walks off that stage each year, though, we have to see the high altitude picture, a perception that can give us some context. Each year, we send another "generation" of adults away from our classrooms. We don't expect them to show up at the classroom door in August. We have done what we were supposed to do.

Another generation out there. We had them walking our hallways, parking in our parking lots, and playing on the playground. For so long, we watched them grow. They were handed to us for a while and now they're gone. A generation.

With that kind of responsibility, we must look at it in a serious and sobering way. Yes, it's fun and it's challenging. It's got its cool moments and general sense of well-being. It can be funny, lighthearted, and leave you feeling good and tired at the end of the day. It's the best way to spend your time. Never forget that this is fun and funny.

But it's also a high level of responsibility. This is a generation and we just let them walk out the gymnasium door. For a time, we can keep up with them, hear about them, even act surprised and pleased when they show up sometime between Thanksgiving and Christmas for that sentimental walk down the hallway, poking their heads in our classroom door just to say hello, experiencing their first shot at nostalgia. But by all rights, they're gone. Another generation.

Let's use our time wisely. Let's not waste this opportunity. We have them for years and whatever else we may do related to passing on information and knowledge, let's see ourselves in a huge way. Let's deserve that good file in their heads. Let's be shepherds.

Don't be guilty of low-level thinking by saying that there's an implication here that students are sheep. That's not what's meant here and anyone should know that. Our reference is solely to define teachers, not students. Anyone who works with kids knows that they are far from being sheep or even sheep-like.

Students are the generations of leaders that will structure and lead society, but there is a learning portion of their life when they must be given the major, classical foundation of knowledge and if that is to be empowering, shepherds are the most important element necessary for the process.

Rather than being *one* of the roles or definitions, this book states that a shepherd is everything a teacher must be, and should be, now. If we move from task-oriented traditional environments toward personalized and broad investments of the wealthy engagement of passionate teachers, the *teacher as shepherd* paradigm is the greatest thing a teacher can be.

WHAT IS A SHEPHERD?

If we are shepherds, we have to make some distinctions that are relevant to the concept and why it's important to understand how it fits with a new, digital transformed learning paradigm. First, we should get the concept right.

If you try to research shepherds, it becomes a difficult task. The history of shepherds is interesting. The difficult element is that it's hard to find too much about the role outside biblical literature. Now, we will address this, but applying the shepherd paradigm to teaching is not simply a biblical application.

There most surely may be some who will point that finger and think that's what's happening here. And there are some characteristics from biblical foundations that are relevant but, for our purposes, we are addressing digital environments in education, current teaching, and learning process.

So it's more than the biblical understanding. It's important to not isolate this concept as a religious argument. We have to go beyond any preconceived ideas and not jump to any conclusions about what we are after here. We look at the role of shepherd because what the shepherd is and does is significant to good teaching in the transformed education environment.

THE FACILITATOR IN TRANSFORMED SYSTEMS

So much of the language about blended learning and environments leveraging technology relegates the role of a teacher to a *facilitator*, someone who makes sure the computer is turned on and running correctly, a pseudo–IT genius. Or at least someone who has the IT genius on speed dial. So often, when we hear the "guide on the side" reference, we demean the role of the teacher as someone who isn't necessarily needed to impart knowledge, information, wisdom, or anything else. Just make sure the lab is operating and the software is doing its job.

That's the wrong picture. We are not facilitators, if that's only defined based on the definitions levied on it by the old teaching systems. In the rush to push lectures out the door (and we should), we can become guilty of going to an extreme that subtracts all the gifted, skilled, and beneficial qualities of good teachers from the classroom.

Teachers are not just facilitators that ensure smooth operating technology and stay out of the way. Neither should they be lecturers who care most about preparing lesson plans and delivering their daily dose of podium magic. There's a balanced approach to teaching.

The world of teaching has changed. The conventional factory system of education has transformed, or at least it's on the way to transforming. As digital environments become the standard and personalized learning becomes the norm, teachers are not to be replaced or eliminated from the classroom. And, just as important, what they do in that classroom is not simply to make sure the computers run on time.

There is a sacred, balanced approach, and we can define it by looking at the *teacher as shepherd* paradigm. Technology doesn't replace teachers. Rather, it repositions teachers in the classroom. And while that's been a long time coming, it's here and its possible now.

THE DEVELOPMENT OF THE SHEPHERD IN LIFE

So let's look at how this fits. In ancient times, as societies progressed, agriculture and farming became important. And in places like Asia Minor, there rose a great need for individuals to watch over large flocks and herds of domesticated animals, particularly sheep. These shepherds would watch over, protect, and care for the flock.[1] Two things are interesting here.

First, the primary responsibility of a shepherd was often the movement of the sheep, the single greatest thing they had responsibility for, *from one pasture to another*. These were unfenced lands, with little to no boundaries. It was necessary to move the sheep across unfenced properties for grazing and shearing. This task would not fall to the owner of the animals. The owners would commit this work to shepherds.

An interesting reason for referring to educators as shepherds is because digital generations will require empowerment, thereby removing most of the fences that have confined them in traditional systems. Shepherds were significant in unfenced territories in earlier times.

Because the fences didn't exist, shepherds were required to move herds from one pasture to another without losing any, keeping them from harm, thus giving them the freedom they needed to benefit from the new pastures they would find. It was systematic and organized. How to allow freedom with no fences while still getting from one place to a better place? Shepherds.

Second, most of the time, *the shepherd was not the owner*. The shepherd took on the responsibility of the sheep but, at the end of the day, did not have ownership. Much like teachers. Parents have always been in charge. Though many believe that teachers take over as parents, this isn't the best scenario.

We may love our students but we are not the parent. Just as shepherds take on so much responsibility *but don't have ownership*, much of the same concept exists between parents and teachers when it comes to learners. That parent knows more and loves more when it comes to his or her child. But we, as teachers, take on so much responsibility for their children. Shepherds.

THREE IMPORTANT CONNECTIONS OF SHEPHERDS

1. The **cultural connection** of economics, survival, and change. In the Neolithic revolution, there were no fences. The farmers owned the sheep and had everything invested. But the farmers didn't move the sheep from pasture to pasture, so the shepherd industry was created.[2] The shepherd took over the responsibility of the sheep. And these people had to be good at it, had to be professional at it, and had to be willing to stand in place of the farmer during those seasons.

    In other words, they had to "adopt" the same connection to the sheep as the farmer during those seasons to move from one place to another—a great picture of the teacher and parent positions when it comes to the child.

    If these students are to move from one place to a better place, we cannot drive them there with rods or lead them there with ropes. Shepherds don't use the rod to drive sheep, they use it to protect them. Shepherds don't pull the sheep along at the end of ropes and leashes.

    Shepherds lead by their voice. To be that voice means that you spend an incredible amount of time with those sheep. A shepherd engages. And the shepherd leads by his or her voice.

    This is us. We must engage the way a shepherd leads. And that requires a genuine connection with our learners. We have to give them the freedom that the digital generations now have but we have to be engaged. Economically, we will benefit with generations of digital students who had good shepherds engaged with them as they moved forward in their learning.

2. The **biblical connection** of love, protection, and legacy for the future. So now we get to it. You can't talk about shepherds without

ancient writings, particularly biblical writings, being your source for information and understanding. It's nothing to apologize for or run from.

In biblical writings, shepherds are portrayed often and are chosen in some significant ways because of the nature of the concept. They are seen as those who love and care for those they shepherd. They protect the sheep.

They stand in for the owner but they believe in their heart that they stand between the sheep and anything that would be harmful. Oh, that every teacher would see this paradigm and act in this manner toward every student every day. Rather than being something that we avoid, we should run to that perception and embrace that as the best part of what we do.

3. The **emotional connection** of ownership, accountability, and responsibility. Rather than the self-esteem movement of *you can change the world* because there is no objective truth and everyone's opinion is equal and right, we have to mentor, apprentice, and teach morality, character, and expectations for generations of learners with a future citizenry in mind.

    And rather than the teacher-controlled environments that defined the industrial systems of the former century, digital learning systems will demand student empowerment. The teacher as shepherd will have to commit emotionally to every student in accountability and responsibility and in making sure the right things are taught.

    Wisdom and morality. These are not terms and concepts that should be abandoned in our public school classrooms. We have to regain and restore moral education and wisdom. These are not reserved just for private school or religious institutions. It's not about religion. It's about a classical curriculum being taught that's founded on the elements of virtue. That's an emotional connection and commitment.

So let's talk about teachers as shepherds and how that relates to a digital world. Education is transforming. We developed a factory model back when the words "factory model" were significant and welcome. During the Industrial Revolution, we developed a system of teaching that was necessary to manage huge populations of students. There was no problem with the system and it worked well.

Every community was connected emotionally, physically, and theoretically to a district school system. That was a huge bureaucracy, but it was also a sense of identity, from large urban areas to small towns in every state.

The issue was that, somewhere in the middle of the past century, we shifted the idea of this model to a paradigm of thought that convinced us that this was the optimum learning environment for students. And as concern grew over the need for more personalized opportunities for learning, the teaching system dug in and wouldn't budge.

So much so that, when there was obvious change needed toward the end of the century, the system was so entrenched that we started tinkering but never transforming anything. Education reform became a natural and expected thought pattern for every educator, policy maker, and community member.

But we are transforming. The change is occurring everywhere. Everyone speaks of transformation now. We are shifting away from a paradigm of education reform; the thought that we can reform something that needs transformation has slowly died away and educators see that transforming from the entrenched teaching system to responsive learning systems is possible now. There was nothing wrong with that in the past but our future stares us in the face.

In mastery-based learning systems, we have the opportunity to perform eight of the nine teaching tasks that were once demanded of busy teachers. Those tasks fenced in our greatest resource in the classroom, our passionate teachers who just wanted to change lives and make a difference every day in the life of a kid.

This left one task undone most of the time: the connection with the learner, the engagement that changed lives and made a difference. All of us have stories about those connections. But now, with personalized learning systems, we can spread that connection further and get it out to every kid.

The greatest wealth we have in our future is sitting in our classrooms today. Teachers seem to know this. Those students will become our adults. That's the wealth of a nation. Teachers seem to know this. And letting technology do what technology can do allows us to finally tap into that greatest resource.

Investing in that resource uncovers that wealthy potential that exists in every young mind. Teachers are investors and they've only needed the time and freedom to invest. We can, and will, get a phenomenal return on that investment if we just keep moving forward in this transformation. *Teachers know they can't rewrite the past but they can rewrite the future for every kid.*

The danger is that there seems to be this "pushing over to the side of the room" of the teacher. And that becomes truth if we believe, or ever believed, that a teacher was only significant as a lecturer, a mere planner and deliverer of content. In that scenario, the teacher, being robbed of that job, certainly would no longer be needed and it would not be necessary for a lecturer to show up.

So there's been a lot of talk about teachers being facilitators. In other words, "we don't need you anymore but we need an adult to make sure the machines are running and, since you have a license and certificate, we want you to expertly facilitate everything. But don't get in the way." It's as if we had a teaching system and now that we changed to a learning system, why would we need teachers? We can get it done without them. But we do need somebody. And we do have them. So let's have them facilitate. *Move to the side, stay out of the way, and facilitate.*

All that's good and well until we realize that the role of a teacher has been around forever. And we're not talking about the 1800s forever. Teaching has been an established part of life for centuries. It's not something that just suddenly appeared to accommodate the factory model of education. Teaching is ageless. There are countless numbers among us who truly believe they can change the world by investing themselves in children and adolescents. That's how they leave their legacy.

In a personalized learning system, designed to focus on the learner, the last thing we should want is to have teachers be facilitators, if that's following the *turn it on and get out of the way* definition. The one task that changes lives is engagement with learners. And the busyness of the other tasks only allowed a small portion of time for that in our classrooms. It was always the thing we did when we had time. Well, now we have time.

We have an engagement environment being created on our campuses and in our classrooms, if we only understand that, instead of relegating teachers to a leftover status where we have to just come up with something for them to do, we go for our best opportunity to get the best from them. *This is the opportunity to be what you wanted to be when you wanted to be a teacher.* Engagement. It changes the lives, it invests in the wealth, and it increases everything for every kid every day.

There's a tremendous need to understand what we need our teachers to do in our new systems. There may always be, at least for an interim time, those educators who hang on to the paradigm of themselves as controllers of the classroom, refusing to change their thinking and digging in even further. That thinking will move those in that generation to a disenfranchised status eventually, as education transforms to student-driven environments.

And there may also be some who will attempt to predefine the role of teachers in a transformed system, get there before everyone catches up, as facilitators and add-ons in classrooms that erases the high level engagement of our educators.

Somewhere in the middle is the truth. Actually, it's not the middle of anything. It's doing what we've always needed to do in education, what has always needed doing but factory models just didn't make possible. Managing large populations of students in an organized system didn't allow it. It's possible now, though, to benefit from the adults who want to spend their day investing in kids.

CONSCIENTIOUS ENGAGEMENT

The engagement with students is the key element to benefit from a transformed learning system. Many have been pushing for transformation for years and the obvious reasons define that push:

1. It minimizes negative effects of comparing bad versus good teachers.
2. It gives more opportunities for progress to more students.
3. It frees up time for career and college preparation.
4. It provides choice for parents and students.
5. It gives more assistance to students needing more assistance.
6. It allows capable students to accelerate their progress.
7. It focuses on learning more than teaching.

There are many more reasons why a transformed learning system, based on mastery learning, is optimal for education. The most significant benefit that becomes possible in this system, though, is what we can now experience in classrooms because we have unleashed our educators from the busy tasks that previously consumed their day. We can now experience true authentic engagement between educators and students, engagement for more students every day.

What does that engagement look like? As we consider, let's briefly review why that engagement is possible now.

In former systems of education, we could perform tasks. The checklist of the tasks took up the time we should have been shepherding. So the best among us shepherded but only as much as time would allow. And the paradigm of good/bad teacher was significant. Not to be too simplistic here, but reading a content lesson, replicating a creative presentation, and assigning/grading homework isn't the highest-level work.

While there may be some merit to a person who can connect with an audience, presentations can be learned and performed. That isn't the magic of the classroom. And even in the situations in which the presentation is engaging, it's the shepherd heart teacher that could inspire even more.

The former teaching systems were task heavy. Educators had a lot to do and not a lot of room was left for connecting with kids.

THE NINE TASKS OF A BUSY TEACHER[3]

While there are so many additional duties of teachers every day, a factory model management system required the following tasks every day:

Lesson planning

This is a large chunk of time spent planning the presentation. During the lesson planning, there is no engagement with the learner, just planning the presentation and organizing the day's delivery of the content.

Lesson preparation

This is a large chunk of time spent preparing and getting everything together to accomplish the planning for the day's presentation of the content. Again, no engagement with the learner, just preparation.

Lesson presentation

This is done within the time framework when students are sitting before us, the presentation of the content, the culmination of those large chunks of time spent planning and preparing. The content is delivered to the group and there's not a lot of genuine, personalized engagement with individual learners. It's a class thing, a group dynamic.

* *Assigning the work to reinforce the content*

This is an administrative piece that should help the group of learners deepen what they've been taught. Once again, there is no personalized engagement with a learner. The assignments are another group dynamic.

* *Assessing the work to measure performance on the assignment*

This is a student-by-student assessment to see how each scores on the assignment. There is no engagement with the learner as this is supposed to be objective. For reasons discussed elsewhere, this sometimes isn't possible, but the nature of assessing work should be that it's objective. But still, the engagement with the learner isn't evident.

* *Grading the assignment*

This is task heavy and time consuming. Some would say this is the same as assessment, but it isn't. Grades become the most subjective result of assessments and it's unfair to give this the heightened sense of sacredness it's never deserved. And as typical, there is no engagement with the learner.

* *Providing feedback to the learner that helps him or her improve*

Sadly this often becomes something that seems to be a choice for teachers. The amount of feedback can be absent or outside of the expectations of some teachers. The excuse is that a teacher cannot be expected to seriously give such a time-consuming task too much attention, especially if that one task steals so much time from the other supposedly important tasks it takes to be a real teacher. Oh, by the way, this task is defined by a true authentic engagement with every learner.

In the transformed system, we will be able to create an engagement environment for teachers that was not possible before. This is what we've needed and what we will need. Technology has the ability to perform the first eight tasks, leaving our teachers better positioned to focus on students, all students.

So we have to rise higher than the thought that teachers become mere facilitators off to the side. We need teachers to take those elements of engagement they've had from the day they first wanted to be a teacher, leverage the technology in the classroom, and invest themselves in our students.

The engagement is high level. In the next chapter, we will discuss in more detail why this is needed, but for now, let's identify this engagement. What we will need from teachers is what we call *conscientious engagement* with students.

Let's define the term and the reasons for the term. "Conscientious" is derived from the Latin meaning "governed by conscience; controlled by or done according to one's inner sense of what is right; principled; careful and painstaking; particular; meticulous application to the work at hand."

Wisdom is more important than information. While appreciating content, to have all the information and no wisdom doesn't serve you well. In a transformed learning system, it becomes very important to teach wisdom to generations of children.

SHEPHERD HEART TEACHERS

In the systems management factory model of education, we demanded accountability in completing the tasks. Anytime you have a checklist system of bureaucratic management, it's simple to check the list, check off the list, and go back to check again at the end of the year to determine if that teacher is meeting expectations. *Sadly, we often forget to check on the kid.* Accountability for teachers can be summed up by checking the checklists. What an organized, neat paper trail we could have.

We've often stated that "you can only expect what you inspect." That usually means the checklist. At the end of the day, though, nobody inspects the heart of a kid. And that's tough to do. We take an organized bell-driven, marching order environment, shove adolescents into it, busy them up with homework, monitor their every move, and expect them to thrive.

And we expect them to behave and be engaged. And because it's easy to inspect behavior, we stick with that. And if they meet our expectation of behavior, we call that engagement. They are here so they're engaged. If they stop coming, they're now disengaged.

That's a dysfunctional, damaging, and destructive paradigm when we talk about the generations of leaders and citizens of our nation. Rather than thriving, they survived us. Now, it's significant that older generations who lead us have gone through this factory model and lead us well. We've always been survivors.

Shepherd heart teachers have always been around. They don't like the model any more than the kids do. And their ability to work outside the model, through the model, and in spite of the model changed lives consistently. But not enough. Not as many.

Digital generations are different. Nothing will be and become more important than conscientious engagement. This element of teaching will be the foundation for all we do and the anchor for why we do it. In previous generations, the systems management held kids highly accountable for attendance and counted that as engagement.

Location-specific paradigms that took a low road for wisdom and gave a false sense that we were successful because everybody showed up. And the highest anecdotes of engagement that had been injected into the process told story after story of individual accounts of shepherd heart teachers who imparted wisdom and conscientious engagement that changed lives, one at a time.

But transformed systems remove location-specific elements and delivery-controlled elements. The good thing is that shepherd heart teachers will do what they've done but so much more than before because the new learning systems will give the freedom for it. More kids being engaged. More lives changed.

The bad thing is that so many educators may do one of two things: 1) refuse to seize the opportunity to become architects in the classroom knowing they can probably get by with minimal engagement during this transitional period between old systems and new; or 2) buy into the facilitator argument and accept a low bar for themselves in the classroom.

Wisdom is crucial. But we've spiritualized the word and the concept so much that it sounds religious. And because we have a misunderstood approach to religion and education in much of the public realm, we look at wisdom as something that exists outside the content and, therefore, not a high priority.

Shepherd heart teachers continue pushing. Teaching wisdom consistently. Mastery learnings systems will demand more than facilitators, but rather conscientious engagement, initiated by the educator, with every learner.

What are the qualities of conscientious engagement? It's important to know that intentional engagement from some may always have some inherent warnings, primarily in the area of personal agendas. It seems that some look for opportunities to replicate themselves, their biases, their thinking, and their feelings.

Shepherd heart teachers don't do that. Shepherd heart teachers construct a solid, trustworthy wisdom paradigm that brings out the best in their students, imparting wisdom that has beneficial qualities, creating within their learners a healthy view of their world and their place in that world.

If we eliminate the personal agendas and biases, what qualities should we see in conscientious engagement? At the top of the list would be those qualities that ensure learners leave us with a personal efficacy to carve their own path. On the day they walk off that stage, have we imparted wisdom? Have we used our time wisely?

If so, we will define that conscientious engagement with balance, diligence, steadfastness, and cautious moderation. We will teach kids to consider thoughtfully those things they will be challenged with. We will not raise our own personal agenda flags to produce miniature, younger versions of ourselves. Rather, we will give them a balanced, steadfast approach to their world.

THE REBELLION OF A SHEPHERD HEART

The head and heart of a shepherd don't exist in other people the same as others. True shepherds have an empathy that thinks like the child. Most shepherds instinctively know the negative effects of tracking, competitive and comparison learning tactics, and standardizing the student.

The shepherd may feel this in the heart but, even more importantly, knows this in the head. The logic of empathy, to feel what a child feels, understands that so many things can hurt a kid, and they won't do those things in their classrooms.

The interesting thing about shepherds is that they rarely administer, practice, or teach things to children that they instinctively "know" will hurt kids, even when mandated to do so in their classrooms. At the end of the day, if a shepherd knows it's harmful, the shepherd won't do it. That's been the good thing about shepherds for years. The shepherd has a head that follows the heart. And the heart is with the child.

The heart of a shepherd is always for the learner. The heart of a shepherd wants every student to succeed, not because it's the natural outcome we should go for in our classrooms but because they personally feel it's the natural outcome for their life's work, their commitment, and their sacrifice. They champion the kid. They believe in the kid. That's the heart of a shepherd.

Shepherds work with kids, as many as possible, to restore, repair, and rescue. These adults knew when they were young they wanted to change the world through teaching. And the work of rescuing kids, restoring relationships, and repairing broken things in kids' lives is genuine, passionate, and demanding. Shepherds meet that demand.

These are not facilitators. These are not lecturers. We did not have a teaching system that idolized the lecturer, transform to a learning system that focuses on the kid, only to have passionate shepherds get to the room to turn the lights on, fire up the computers, and sit on the sidelines to facilitate.

Rather than thinking of how to move teachers out of the way, we need to leverage this transformed opportunity to get the best out of these shepherds. And once we understand even a very small part of the world of digital generations, we will understand why shepherds are needed more than ever.

NOTES

1. A. González-Ruibal and M. Ruiz-Gálvez, "House Societies in the Ancient Mediterranean (2000–500 BC)," *Journal of World Prehistory* 29, no. 4 (2016): 383–437, doi:10.1007/s10963-016-9098-8.

2. S. Bréhard, A. Beeching, and J. Vigne, "Shepherds, Cowherds and Site Function on Middle Neolithic Sites of the Rhône Valley: An Archaeozoological Approach to the Organization of Territories and Societies," *Journal of Anthropological Archaeology* 29, no. 2 (2010): 179–88, doi:10.1016/j.jaa.2010.02.001.

3. A. Wimberley, *Reshaping the Paradigms of Teaching and Learning: What Happens Today Is Education's Future*, first ed. (Lanham, MD: Rowman & Littlefield, 2016).

2

THE WORLD OF DIGITAL GENERATIONS

THE GAME HAS CHANGED

Wisdom. We haven't found the technology, the app, or the program that teaches wisdom. And we won't. Wisdom is transferred from generation to generation. When we gather young generations of children and adolescents together into a building, when we tether them together with wireless connections around the world, when we sit with them in our living rooms, hopefully we know enough to know that we teach them more than science, reading, and math. Wisdom isn't something to be trifled with. It's the most significant thing we have and we transfer it from one generation to the next.

Sadly, in the systems of teaching we are transforming from, the teacher wasn't always able to be a shepherd transferring wisdom because there wasn't time. But in the transformed learning systems we can experience now, we can be true shepherds. And we can ensure that mature wisdom is passed on to those who will lead us one day.

That's never been more important than it is now because the world is changing, and has changed, more for digital generations than ever before. To be shepherds now is to feel the weight of the calling and the responsibility. We need shepherd heart teachers.

We now live in a digital world. Those of us who would be considered nondigital don't necessarily thrive in this world, but we get along just fine. Rather than fighting it, we download as best we can. We appreciate it, we use it, and we marvel at it. We depend on it so much because we have to depend on it so much.

Our bank forces us to depend on it. Our job forces us to depend on it. Our kids force us to depend on it. When presented with the question, "How did we ever get along without it?" the nondigital generation usually replies that we got along just fine without it. But it's here to stay and we get along with it too.

There are some, much younger, who have been in the middle of technology expansion, as it moved from computers to digital, and have been first adopters, fast trackers, and fluent users of digital capacity. They are probably still considered "old school" in some ways but are way ahead of the older generations who just get by the best they can.

These are the sandwich generations who remember landline phones but watched them fade away. To these generations, there's no nostalgic remembrance of a "car phone." They just know they can use a phone while driving now.

The digital generations are in an entirely different world. Our grandchildren are texting, posting, and tapping their way through this life. Preschoolers are routinely handed a digital device to entertain, enlighten, and engage them throughout the day. Parents intentionally train their child to "x" out of the ads and commercials popping up in apps and games to ensure there's no accidental purchases. In the beginning, there was an effort to decry the moral dilemma of using technology as a babysitter, but even that is disappearing as digital becomes life.

No longer do we make distinctions of digital natives and immigrants [1] as we've now moved into second and third digital generations. We are not moving into the land of digital; we've settled and colonized in this land and technology has a manifest destiny that won't stop until all corners of our culture are occupied and living comfortably within its borders.

It's just simpler now to refer to the distinctions as *digital* and *nondigital* generations. The nondigitals are being left alone, left behind, or left out in this progress. They are not ignorant, just ignored. And soon the nondigitals will die out and only digitals will be left.

None of this is a moral outcry. Rather, it's a wake-up call to be more attentive than alarmed. Digital technology is us. And as we dive deeper into the cultural aspects, there will come a point that forces a reality check. When we consider the promises promised right now, it's important to know that technology won't replace life.

Innovations and progress promise everything, but there comes a moment when the reality of what these can't do levels the progress out and settles the innovations down. We have no flying cars, though dreams and promises of such were advertised when automobiles first rode into town long ago.

This reality check will not cause a decline in technology usage or proliferation but will slow the progress and bring a common sense utilization that informs the culture going forward. However, that reality check isn't here yet and isn't scheduled to arrive for quite a while. Our digital generations will thrive in this digital world as adults.

So what do we do? We, those who educate, teach, and lead these generations of children. How can we best use our time with these learners wisely? *Wisdom.* If we do not shepherd, these generations could possibly have all information at their fingertips, all knowledge on their screens, but no wisdom in their heart and minds.

The subject matter and content in our courses may never change. Students will learn what they must learn. But transferring wisdom is so significant because, left with no shepherding, we can end up creating a world in which the moral center becomes so self-focused, even to the point of detriment to others and a consuming protection of the self.

We naturally love ourselves and are constantly processing a self-centered existence. We have to learn character (how we act) and morality (what we believe). Wisdom is the knowledge that informs and guides our behavior.

The particular significance in the digital world is that technology has now created some tremendous conditioning challenges for younger generations. So much information, so many rants, intrusive and widespread, are now offered to our children every day simply because of the connectedness of the digital environment.

The idea that ideas are to be rewarded and respected wholesale, while tolerance is the greatest character trait to possess, injects itself in the stream of constant information that is delivered, offered, or forced on our children through technology. *To believe everything is dangerous and to accept everything is dangerous.*

Some would say that anyone who would protect children from exposure to all ideas and information may simply be afraid to trust children and adolescents to have the capacity to process all this. And faced with that accusation, we should admit that fear.

There are multitudes of ideas and opinions that are harmful for children and adolescents and they must not be trained or bullied to accept or tolerate these. Without a shepherd, without wisdom, they can be conditioned to things that will affect their lives as adults. And the digital world creates the platform that can lead to this conditioning.

For our purposes, we will not dig too deep. Much research, at highly intellectual levels, is being conducted on the neurological, social, academic, and behavioral consequences and effects of digital environments.[2] In our society, the technology that has shaped how we operate and interact has completely changed so much and studies abound. However, our primary purpose is to target that classroom, point out some conditions of a digital life that affect our learners in that classroom, and focus on the significance of the shepherd for those learners.

CULTURAL CONDITIONING FOR DIGITAL GENERATIONS

The world of digital technology is redefining communication. While it's a given that we are all basically the same, with shared elements of life common among us, it's always been understood that we are vastly different and unique in so many ways.

The concept of community between people is one of the challenges of life simply because no two people are exactly alike and the plethora of ideas and opinions among even very small groups of individuals can be difficult to maneuver and navigate. Creating community is a worthy pursuit of life but it's challenging for all of us.

There seems to be a common thread that runs through much thinking that the perfect environment is one in which every idea and opinion is afforded the same credibility and given equal status. This dismisses the value of discernment and labels those who won't buy into the thinking as being intolerant. It's as if we are marching toward a perfected society and anyone who might stop or slow down in a cautionary way is out of step.

None of this is new. We've always had the uniqueness of people making life interesting. And in our own living rooms, that uniqueness plays itself out constantly. Even families want to go home to their own living rooms after spending just a short period of time at the annual family reunion. It's a sense that, while appreciating, loving, and tolerating the vastly different ideas between people, there is still that part of us that doesn't accept everything.

The automobile is a sufficient example for showing how a cultural progression caused greater challenge. As the car is the mode of transportation used most widely in society, watch what happens when too many of these get on the road and start moving around together in traffic. Those vehicles are only machines of steel. They have no personality and no thoughts of their own. It's not the cars out there on the road. It's us.

Get enough of us trying to get somewhere at the same time, with our opinions and perceptions, and see what happens in traffic. Multiple dramas are played out from the driver's seat. Perceptions and attitudes are controlling steering wheels.

That highway, those ribbons of concrete, and that incessant traffic are a meeting place where everything that normally stays in our own living rooms comes together. It's a cultural collection rather than a cultural connection. And that collection doesn't always end well.

CULTURAL COLLECTIONS

In a digital world, the internet has built a new house. One of the greatest set of studies being performed in research is how to create connections in online environments.[3] The capacity to feel connected is given the highest priority for those who are studying online learning and social media.

But the digital environments of social media appear to be redefining communication while simultaneously forcing every idea, opinion, and perception out of every living room and crashing them together on an invisible cloud somewhere.

And it's certainly more a *cultural collection* rather than a *cultural connection*. There's tremendous difference between the two. However, in a world in which young people are being pushed to accept everything and tolerate all things, the cultural collection presents itself as the world they should accept and tolerate at all costs.

Even the iconic trademarks of digital communication want to replace some elemental requirements for genuine, authentic, and understood language. What we say isn't always what they heard. And it's necessary to use body language, genuine transparency, and thoughtful "presence" when communicating.

The elements of an overwhelming social media world disseminated through devices eliminates that presence, as well as that sense of accountability one feels when present during the communication. Say anything. Say it however you want. And once said, click out and you don't have to face any immediate consequence.

It's a typing world. So we replace true emotion in the interaction with emojis. We have so many tiny faces to somehow let everybody know how we feel—how we feel about people and how we feel about what we said or what someone else said. Cute little cartoon image letting the world know how we feel.

When we have presence in a social interaction, the immediate reaction or response from an individual is affected by the body language, the inflection and nuance, and the felt emotion. How something is said is just as important as what is said. Why something is said affects how it's received.

Often, what we say may not be what they heard. Immediate reaction from the listener in the conversation is largely affected by these elements of physical presence and the tactical modifications in our language with each other.

Though some want to believe that the digital paradigm of communication is connected, it's disconnected from the element of presence. One of the most significant aspects of presence is that of accountability. We are standing there, we are in the room. Or on the phone.

And there's a sense of accountability because we have that check in ourselves that holds us back or pushes us forward because of it. In the digital world, we just hit "send" and it's out there. Accountability in social media doesn't exist or is, at the very least, diminished to a point of little significance to navigate conversations, monologues, or personal rants. We hit "send," click out, and move on.

PERCEPTIONS WITHOUT PRESENCE

Meanwhile, our words, topped off with a cute emoji, are traveling through some cloud atmosphere, seen and read by everybody, anybody, or nobody. But the immediate reaction of those reading it won't have the benefit of your presence to ask for clarification, to seek understanding, or to discover more of your meaning from further dialogue. Communication becomes a bumper sticker mentality. "Let the world know who I am and they can love it or leave it."

The problem is that digital communication and social media want to hold the highest place in our culture. Refusing to take a back seat because it offers so much engagement, it grows and grows until it redefines what we've come to expect from communication, social interaction, and expressing ourselves. Everybody's got the bumper sticker and everybody's reading my bumper sticker. So get that message about me out there.

But it's not supposed to replace human engagement or primary social interactions. Digital generations are growing up in a world in which this consuming paradigm of conversation has the appearance of holding the highest place in our culture.

It's often thought that what we think about ourselves doesn't necessarily dictate how we react and respond. And what someone thinks of us doesn't necessarily dictate how we react and respond. *But it's what we think someone thinks about us that dictates how we react and respond to others.*

Perception. In a social interaction, as we communicate with someone, our mind is processing our perception of how that person feels about us and that image we form of that perception. It can produce anger that may be unfounded, inappropriate emotional reactions, and uncalled-for misunderstandings.

In the digital world, if the typing and the typed message is the only message, then it is the victim of perception and processing. What we say may not be what they heard. Nondigital generations still understand that surely that message has much more to it than the simple words showing on the screen.

But the point of this chapter is to reinforce why nondigital generations have to be shepherds to digital generations. These younger generations have not seen the progress and the layered growth of this environment. *They've known nothing but this environment.* We have to be shepherd heart teachers teaching wisdom.

THE SELF-ESTEEM CONDITION

There's no doubt and no argument that we must have a healthy, aggressive, and expressive love for children if we are to be teachers. We have to first love the generations we teach. So much of the time, we are not confronted with the question of whether we love children or not.

That question is not asked nor are we often challenged about it. But make no mistake, we only need adults who love children doing this work. *When that door closes and that adult is alone with those students, it must be someone who loves our children.*

And for those who love children, our greatest hope is that they have a good and positive sense of themselves. Nondigital generations didn't necessarily have teachers focused on building the self-esteem in us. We had nice teachers and some not so nice teachers. Everyone knew who the nice teachers were and everybody definitely knew who the not so nice teachers were.

The sandwich generations, though, were part of an aggressive self-esteem movement. Suddenly, pats on the head become a teacher move. Everybody got ribbons and everybody won because it might hurt someone's feelings. And hurting someone's feelings was not acceptable. So rather than teaching true characteristics of resilience and determination, it became easier to just make them feel good about themselves. Tell them it's all about them.

Tolerance became the greatest character trait. Everyone is right and the world is big enough to hold everyone as right. Maybe the world is big enough, but when it scales back down to that one twenty-by-thirty-foot classroom, the "everybody's right" collides and confuses.

When generations of children are taught to be tolerant of everything, they do it at the expense of the character trait of discernment. To be discerning is paramount to character and morality. We should always be tolerant. We should always be kind. And we should always love people first. But we must also be discerning.

We must know that not everything is good and not everyone is right. But for the sake of tolerance, we give up our rights of discernment and it can become difficult to navigate as an adult. And that can lead to an entire cultural shift.

If we now have adults who have sacrificed discernment, whether it's because of personal belief or cultural pressure, and we are now teaching digital generations, we have to take a step back and see the effects of these two variables. So much information, so many ideas, and so much thrown at these digital generations—expressions, attitudes, and opinions intruding every day on young learners.

There is an inherent tension between tolerance and discernment. Yes, we must be tolerant. But even more, we must be discerning. We must move away from simply patting kids on the head, telling kids that everything is okay and right, allowing them to be inundated with every possible thought without teaching them wisdom.

We need discernment informed by love and concern for others that weighs the ideas and information carefully and considers the information thoughtfully. And we need the bravery to not be pressured to believe that everything is right. Digital generations are growing up in a world in which everything will be presented and tolerated because digital technology provides it. We have to be shepherd heart teachers teaching wisdom.

THE CONSISTENT UNREST

In the digital world, information is available. Information is powerful because it can create a sense of community and shared feelings, the idea that this is a widespread and accepted belief that everyone believes and, therefore, the reader should believe as well. The internet, accessed by everyone, becomes the "print" that presents the information.

But this can cause widespread proliferation of wrong information, bad ideas, and harmful perceptions. That widespread dissemination can instill a consistent unrest. Depending on the motives or intent of the information that is guaranteed broad readership, the digital capacity to distribute everywhere can:

- build disharmony while giving the appearance of bringing people together,
- create a sense of unrest and panic where none is warranted,
- send a message of unity that requires compliance or face expulsion from the mainstream,
- break down independence while requiring a dependence on the community, and
- inform readers that disrespect and rebellion are expected and honorable.

Our young learners should be allowed to be young. And growing up should not be short-circuited or hijacked early by a consistent feeling of unrest. The digital information age of communication, and the fact that this is presented and utilized so much by young learners, can give the appearance that there is a collective panic that they will be touched by because everyone must feel this way and everyone believes this. Tragedies and atrocities have always occurred but they were seen in the past as acts of individual responsibility and violent people. Now they are defined as broad and systemic defects in our nation or community.

Our young learners are presented with the idea that, rather than having individuals in society who can think and act in ways that can be alarming, disrespectful, and dangerous, they are living in a defective cultural society that will somehow personally affect them.

This shapes how these young learners perceive their world and their place in that world. And if that world is seen as defective simply because an isolated act is committed, it can create a stressed and anxious thread that runs through their every thought.

There will always be isolated and individual behavior among people. But every wrong act and wrong idea does not constitute the premise that this occurred because everything is wrong and there is no safe place. Digital generations are being exposed to so much information so much earlier in life.

And while adults understand that, just because someone would have us believe that this isolated act or idea is symptomatic of a systemic and broad national defect doesn't make it so, children may not be able to process this. It creates an internal unrest among our younger generations. We have to be shepherd heart teachers teaching wisdom.

THE VULNERABILITY FACTOR

In the digital world, we trust the internet. As we connect more devices, as we tie more tasks to our bandwidth, and as we plunge deeply into a networked life, even the basic but necessary aspects of that life will be solely dependent on the strength or weakness of the internet. And the capacity of that connected system, whether robust or frail, can determine whether we are able to carry out even the most basic activities of life.

How often do we now hear, "Our system is down"? One can be standing at the checkout counter of the grocery store, ten dollar bill in hand to purchase a six-dollar item, and not be able to walk out with the item if the store's computer is not working properly.

If your network at home disconnects, you can't pay your bills, check on your friends, or respond to emails. Buying groceries, banking, or purchasing fuel for the car and communicating with your friends, your boss, and your family all depend on this.

Staying updated on the weather, the news, and the world, and even finding a restaurant depend on this. From the most mundane to the most complex elements of a daily life, the internet has become the lifeline, the life blood, and the life support that determines whether these things can be done.

This isn't an alarming concept. Nor is it necessarily alarming that the system can break down. Nondigital generations have always known that systems break down. The car breaks down. Things stop working. The roof may sometimes leak and need repair. Those growing up in the nondigital world roll up their sleeves and make it work when the system breaks down. There is no reason to panic because sometimes you have to work around that broken system.

What is alarming, though, is that those growing up in the digital world are being taught a dependence on vulnerable connected systems and may not be equipped to deal with a nonconnected life untethered. There is a tremendous distinction between being nonconnected and disconnected. Nondigital generations don't necessarily feel disconnected and helpless when a system stops working. It happens, and when it does, you just work through it.

But we are teaching digital generations to rely on a vulnerable and fragile system. If we have tied so much of the basic and common necessities in our day to a digital framework, the ability to disrupt, damage, or destroy our capacity to carry out even the fundamental pieces of life depend on the strength of that framework.

And older generations seem to expect a breakdown in the system. And they carry on. Unless we've so connected ourselves that the capacity to work around the system is also stolen from us. We will most likely have that ten dollar bill at the checkout counter. And we are ready to hand it over and walk away with the item.

The term digital distress is beginning to be used and heard around the nation. This term has been used in marketing circles and also in a recent study conducted by the Brookings Institute addressing the unequal distribution of broadband access to various communities and regions.[4]

For our purposes, adding the vulnerability of a system that is increasingly controlling so much of life, then having a generation of life totally dependent on that vulnerable system, digital distress could also be used to describe the effects on a culture and life if it has never learned to get by without it. These digital generations are consumed with the internet. Because it's all they've known, what will be their reaction if it disappeared?

The alarming thing for nondigital generations is not that the system is down. *What's alarming is when we are told that common tasks can't be done because a computer somewhere in another part of the country stops churning.*

When you trust a system, that system must be worthy of your trust. Most of the time, nondigital generations trust digital life and expect the inconvenience inherent with the vulnerability of the internet. But what may seem inconvenient for these older generations can be inconceivable to generations that have known nothing but a connected life. And that's where the alarm sets in.

If digital was gone tomorrow, would we survive?

The responses to that question from nondigital generations and digital generations could be vastly different. What if we suddenly couldn't get our money from our bank, buy groceries, or post a picture online? What if our television screen was dark, our thermostats didn't come on, or no one outside the house knew how we were feeling at the moment? What if the cloud broke up, the satellite quit transmitting, and the music stopped streaming?

The problem is not that these things may happen. *The problem is what the response can be if these things happen.* We are relying on a connected system that can be unconnected, nonconnected, or disconnected with the flip of the switch, a tap on the screen, or push of the button. We depend on this to work. But it breaks down. And the system itself has a dependence on particular things happening and not happening to keep working. It works. What if it doesn't? And what if it won't? What happens then?

How would our culture react if we suddenly had a broken internet that wasn't likely to be resolved or repaired within a year? Or within a month or week? What if the entire system broke down across the board for every program, application, and technology for one full day? How would we respond?

Could we return to a day before a digital life? Those of us, and that's all of us, who have been raised in a world of modern convenience would not react well if automobiles were removed from every part of life. It would be inconceivable and damaging, not only physically crippling for business, homes, churches, schools, and life in general, but also to the psyche and the fabric of our culture. Why? Because we've grown up in an automobile world.

We aren't part of nonautomobile generations. Yet a few decades ago, when we had nonautomobile and automobile generations, had the car industry and environments disappeared from life, those who had navigated a world that didn't have automobiles would be better equipped to get along.

Transfer that to digital and nondigital generations. Our current generations of learners are being conditioned to not consider digital capacity as an opportunity to thrive in this world. *Rather, these generations are being conditioned to consider digital capacity as the only way they can survive in this world.*

When these generations of learners become adults, they will lead us. And they will inherit all of this when we are gone. And while it would be nice to believe that digital environments will remain strong and expansive, the ability to disrupt it so easily makes it vulnerable. The digital generations will need wisdom.

Each generation has a dependence on progressive and successive innovations. And maybe there is a day in the future when the internet will be embedded and protected so well and so reliably that its vulnerability is diminished or eliminated. That day may or may not be possible and only the future will tell. Until then, though, we have to be wise.

Digital generations, particularly in social and communication arenas, are being conditioned to depend on a vulnerable way of life that can be manipulated, managed, and mutated by many. And the multiple elements of this everyday life imprint things and concepts that can affect everything. Hard starts and reboots, upgrades and updates, downloading and uploading, unsubscribing, unfollows and disconnects. These are simple things. But they can affect how we see the world, if that's the only world we've known.

Behavior and emotional security, a feeling of safety, can be affected. It's not too alarming if that's occurring in isolated circumstances, times, or people. But the internet is different. Having the ability to reach everyone is great. But that's also the greatest weakness.

If it's so inclusive and widespread, the danger of negative reactions when its vulnerability is exposed can also be inclusive and widespread. That's not something that affects a person; that affects a generation. We have to be shepherd heart teachers teaching wisdom.

TEACHERS AS SHEPHERDS

The myth of modern progression is that history is most likely wrong, less informed, and full of nondeserving heroes who should have their faults and failures paraded out for all to see and judge. The myth is that we are progressing to a better man. Therefore, what has gone before is to be considered lesser and not worthy of honor or serious regard.

And digital generations are growing up in a world in which this message can be manipulated and communicated in a broad way. Culture is being created. We can end up abandoning things that we should never abandon. *And if we can somehow move our teachers to the side, asking them to only facilitate the digital tools, we further remove this generation from our greatest hopes for wisdom being transferred.*

Shepherds know that there are improvements and progress. But the idea that we can abandon classical curriculum content and established truth only works if we are willing to say there are no absolutes in life.

An absolute is an unchangeable truth that remains objective and significant for every generation and informs every generation, no matter how we progress or improve the tools and innovations. Absolutes don't go away simply because some want them to go away.

Intelligence is important. But wisdom and intelligence are separate. Wisdom recognizes absolutes and supports and strengthens absolutes even when the intelligent progress of culture advances. Transferring wisdom to generations demands a strong role for teachers in a transformed learning world.

We are transforming our classrooms from teaching systems to learning systems. And we should. And the leveraging of the tools and resources is necessary. We have opportunities to provide more. But make no mistake. *This is no time for us to relegate teachers to a facilitator role in classrooms, if that means standing off to the side while the computer hums.*

Technology does not replace teachers. Rather, it repositions teachers. And that position is not standing off to the side of the room once the computers are booted up and turned on.

Our children are growing up in a world in which they are smarter than we are when it comes to digital capacity. That world is changing for us but it's all they've known. And while we should know that our best hope is to let technology do what it does, we should also know that content and information has never been all we should be doing in our classrooms.

Consider this:

1. In the industrial teaching system, the teacher was a possessor of information.
2. The delivery of that information was apportioned, planned, and distributed by the teacher.
3. The consuming tasks of teaching systems didn't allow teachers to spend much time transferring wisdom to many students.
4. Technology now provides opportunities to accomplish most of the teaching tasks that formerly consumed a teacher's day.
5. There is a transformation in education from teaching systems to learning systems and teachers are not necessarily viewed as the sole possessors of content and information now.
6. In the transformation, many want to assign a facilitator role to teachers, defined as someone who simply makes sure the technology behaves and operates correctly.
7. If we allow this definition for teachers to become our standard, we will not leverage the best that teachers can offer in our classrooms.
8. A transformed system will position the adult in a classroom to finally engage with more learners, letting technology do what it does best.
9. Now is our most optimum opportunity to accomplish the best we can for digital generations.
10. The best we have for classrooms is having shepherd heart teachers transferring wisdom to digital generations while technology delivers, processes, and measures classical curriculum to our learners.

So what is this wisdom? What would we pass on to generations of learners? If we have intelligent teachers, full of information and knowledge, that's good. But if we have shepherd heart teachers, that's better. What should they transfer to our digital generations?

NOTES

1. S. Wang, H. Hsu, T. Campbell, D. Coster, and M. Longhurst, "An Investigation of Middle School Science Teachers and Students' Use of Technology Inside and Outside of Classrooms: Considering Whether Digital Natives Are More Technology Savvy Than Their Teachers," *Educational Technology Research and Development* 62 (2014): 637–62.

2. L. Laidlaw and J. O'Mara, "Rethinking Difference in the iWorld: Possibilities, Challenges and 'Unexpected Consequences' of Digital Tools in Literacy Education," *Language and Literacy* 17, no. 2 (2015): 59–74.

3. J. Delahunty, I. Verenikina, and P. Jones, "Socio-Emotional Connections: Identity, Belonging and Learning in Online Interactions. A Literature Review," *Technology Pedagogy and Education* 23, no. 2 (2014): 243–65, doi:10.1080/1475939X.2013.813405.

4. A. Tomer, E. Kneebone, and R. Shivaram, "Signs of Digital Distress: Mapping Broadband Availability and Subscription in American Neighborhoods," September 15, 2017, https://www.brookings.edu/research/signs-of-digital-distress-mapping-broadband-availability.

3

THE MORAL EDUCATION PARALLEL FOR THE SHEPHERD HEART TEACHER

Every day across our country, a door closes somewhere around 8:00 a.m. In fact, close to 2 million doors close. Reports state that, in the first semester of the 2016–2017 school year, there were approximately 50.7 million public school students and 5.2 million private school students in America.[1]

Even a rudimentary calculation, using thirty students per classroom, comes to more than 1.8 million doors closing, all at about the same time and all with the same result: learners sitting in that classroom. And that doesn't take into account homeschools across the nation. Those doors are symbols, icons of the tremendous responsibility we have in this nation to educate our young.

What we owe our children is the best opportunity to gather knowledge and information, organize it in a coherent way, and deliver it in such a manner that they learn. Humans learn because we were created to learn. There may be variance in the capacity between individuals, unique abilities, giftedness, or tendencies in the learning process. But we learn.

The system of education in America is a behemoth. It is an industry, a way of life, and an ingrained piece of our psyche. We go to school. And it's organized. It's seasonal, rhythmic, and patterned and we revolve our lives around it. It is embedded in our culture and it controls what, when, and why we do so much of life.

But every life tells a story. And every seat in those classrooms, approximately 55 million, has a student sitting in it. And each one of those students will spend the majority of that day learning. What will they learn from us that day?

THE THINGS WE OWN

We have things that we must pass on to the next generation. While we can't think that we can create an exhaustive list of the volumes of things we pass on, we can look at the headline items. We have three particularly important things they should inherit from us.

Information

You have to know how to get through life. To do that, you have to know things. That seems simple. However, we can be guilty of thinking they know these things when they come to us, when in fact they don't. We have the volume of information we need to pass on.

The beauty of third grade is that these students walk in at the beginning of the year not knowing the information they need to know. The teacher gives them the information throughout the year. It's work and it can be hard work. They don't know this information. Hopefully, the teacher is able to teach this information in a way that makes it a part of their thinking. They gain information. They leave that teacher knowing more than they knew when they came in.

The rhythm of education is that, approximately three months later, a new crew of third-grade learners march into that classroom. Rather than the teacher starting where he or she left off three months before, he or she starts over. These children don't have that information. And he or she will teach it. We have information, we possess it, and they need it. That's a good life: teaching those children the information and handing it off.

If that teacher decided to ignore the newness of the class and just assume the students would get it somehow, a generation of third-graders would have their information banks stunted. In other words, they won't have it and they won't get it. Though it may seem simple, it's a fundamental concept. We possess information and we have to pass it on.

Morality

Often, we believe kids are who they are. We can be guilty of thinking we can't shape behavior, we can only control it. We may believe that a bad kid is a bad kid and always will be. But we can teach a moral center in our classrooms. We can teach a moral center to life.

We have a duty to teach a moral center. They need us to help them learn those things. While we always want to treat students with dignity, gentleness, and compassion, we do them no favors by instilling in them a self-esteem mindset that exists in a vacuum if we have not also taught them that life is about how we have a responsibility toward others. We have that moral center and we can teach it and hand it off to those generations.

Wisdom

This is the one possession we own that must be handed off and can often get lost. Learning is more than a rote, by the number process. Wisdom is knowing how to use the information we gain in life in a way that benefits others and benefits ourselves in good ways.

It's easy to lose sight of the magnitude of our calling. And an organized system of teaching starts, accelerates, coasts, ends, pushes through, and pushes on. And there's so much to learn—math, science, reading, writing, history, and more. And there's so much to do—get them in, start on time, keep them moving, sit them down. Tests, homework, athletics, recess, lunch. Get it all in, every day, and on time. It's so much.

But that door. That door closes and, for each teacher in each classroom, those children are all that matters. That teacher has a sole responsibility to do the best for each child that day. It's important to not lose sight of the magnitude of our calling. Yes, it's an industry and it's a behemoth. But each child in our care deserves our best. We will grow old and we will go away. And what we leave them with will live on. So what do we leave them with?

So many think that our subjects, our content, is the entirety of our possessions. Those various bodies of information that are handed to each generation incrementally, hopefully giving them a solid foundation of knowledge that carries these learners from childhood to adulthood. And hopefully they take their places in our communities, eventually leading us.

They have to have that knowledge just to get along. Though some may never go past the high school diploma and some may never stop their formal learning in higher education, we will depend on each generation to one day take on their responsibilities just as we did.

But is that all we have? Even in the best possible situation, we have an educated, trained, and intelligent adult with a particular interest and knowledge of a particular subject, alone in the classroom controlling the delivery of that information to these students. And that adult most likely has a passion, an internal desire to help these kids.

Somewhere within the mind and heart of that teacher is a driving force that gets them up and gets them into that classroom, day after day. Somewhere in their own learning, as they were growing, they made a decision to be a teacher. And as they stand there in that room, what do they own that they can give?

It's not just the subject matter. It's not just the information, organized and parceled out in a scope and sequence. It's not just those bodies of content material, written in that textbook or appearing on a computer screen. That material exists already and it's existed for so many years.

That adult leads us, stands beside us, and journeys with us as we learn new things. That teacher is often the sole adult in some of our greatest moments. As children play out their daily dramas, endure their greatest hardships, or experience their greatest triumphs, it's likely a teacher accompanying the moment. They are our companions in life during significant stages and ages of our personal growth.

Those in education, those who call themselves teachers, must know what they have to give this generation of learners. And it's so much more than the subject matter. If we define teachers and teaching, we must raise our expectations. And if we see teaching as an intentional, targeted task for a child, then what would we teach? In a world that possesses all the information already, we don't teach that information. We deliver it. We didn't create it and we didn't invent it. So what do we have?

When we work with the young, those who will learn, we have to establish one significant point: *We share information but we teach wisdom and morality.* This is what we have: wisdom and morality. In transformed learning systems, that subject matter can be shared in so many engaging ways, whether it be through technology, lectures prepared by professionals, and more. It's shared and they learn.

But what do we teach? We share information but we teach wisdom and morality. These young learners need us. And by law, they will be with us, every day. Yes, let's share that content, that subject matter. But let's teach wisdom and morality. Teachers should be naturally bent toward a skill in teaching. Teachers should have that passion to teach.

Teachers must feel that sense of responsibility for each learner. And while it may be important to be a subject matter expert, the most important thing we can give them is wisdom and morality. The ability to measure the knowledge they gain with a sense of moral character that will inform them, lead them, and direct their lives.

Teachers will be with children. We spend so much time teaching our teachers to teach. And the bulk of that training will be developing the skills of teaching, the practice and the elements of getting through the day. Do we spend time teaching teachers to teach wisdom and morality? We should because the generational legacy we leave will mark us years from now.

Articulating Wisdom in Education

In 1943, one of the greatest philosophers and writers of the twentieth century, C. S. Lewis, wrote the great work *The Abolition of Man*.[2] Though we are not producing a full review and analysis of the book here (there are many reviews that can be found), we would point out some specific things from the work related to what we discuss at this point.

Lewis was addressing education and the dangers faced should there be a continual shift toward moral relativism in schools. He was concerned that educators were leaving the truths of objective and absolute morals and values that had always been the foundation for teaching the young. In the book, Lewis uses the Tao to identify that set of moral values. He was addressing the idea that learners were being taught that values and moral truths were subjective and could even be replaced. He understood that, no matter how much he may want to, man cannot invent new morals, truths, or values. These are absolute and don't change over time.

We would agree. Even as we find, in a social media digital world, that everyone now has the ability to collide together over the internet, that doesn't mean that everything colliding out there is truth. And we certainly can't invent or create new truth. Man has the ability to create laws and legislation. And ideas run the gamut of opinions.

A full spectrum of reactions and judgments about anything will be found in a digital world. But truth remains constant. While it would be nice to think that we can invent new truth, we would have to fall in line with this great philosopher and admit that this simply can't be done. Shepherd heart teachers know this.

In his book, he referred to the efforts of some in education who were trying to turn the tide of subjective moralism back to an objective center. However, the efforts took the form of trying to eliminate some of the more creative elements of teaching and replacing that creative side of learners with a strict mode of engagement.

That engagement only offered a disciplined approach to everything and left no room for learners to have their passions and emotions ignited in learning. In other words, remove much from the learner and replace it with the strict and disciplined.

Lewis's admonishment refers to "cutting down the jungles" in the learner that shows evidence of anything other than the strictness of disciplined thought, thereby leaving a razed plain for planting. In other words, try to intentionally address those things and spend the time to turn those things around in learners.

Lewis, however, offered a different approach. He called on modern educators to "irrigate deserts." This is a fascinating picture of the instructional process and transferring wisdom to generations. Take them as they are and start there. Pour into those children and adolescents the right thing and the good thing. Irrigate the deserts of the mind and the heart.

This is important for us as we consider how to transfer wisdom to digital generations. The future adults may be living in a world highly controlled and influenced by digital resources and requirements. In that world, they will need to be wise. While they are with us, we should not expend all of our time fighting *against* something (cutting down the jungles of the shifts toward moral subjectivity), we should be spending our time fighting *for* something (irrigating the deserts).

How does that look? It means that shepherd heart teachers will do the good thing every day for every learner. It means shepherd heart teachers will use their time wisely and engage in a way that the foundations of truth and morals will be anchors for the learner, now and in the future. In these efforts, we must take into account some resources and responsibilities we have during this time of educating the young.

MORAL EXEMPLARS

In previous decades, educators who cared intentionally about creating a moral standard for learners would often turn to exceptional exemplary individuals as examples of moral character and action to give these learners someone to emulate. Biographies of these exceptional moral exemplars might be read or assigned as reading projects for students. Men and women who dedicated their lives to the pursuit of creating change for others. And this would have a good effect in the personal moral development of the learner.

Just being exposed to their narratives and stories of personal morality created personal motivation to live that way as well. Abraham Lincoln, Martin Luther King Jr., Mother Teresa, and George Washington were examples of exceptional moral exemplars for young learners. One of Lawrence Kohlberg's theories of moral education was based on this moral exemplarity.[3]

However, in recent years, this has started to change. The latest research shows that just being exposed to these narratives may have a diminished, and even negative, effect now. That's not surprising because our world is changing at such a rapid pace, and current generations are being exposed to so much so much sooner. There may be a disconnect between the reality of today and the isolated narratives of those who represented the models of morality from yesterday.[4]

There is a need to provide those examples though. However, the research seems to lead more to a conclusion that digital learners require a more visible and current example. And while the digital world provides many choices and opinions, we would encourage shepherd heart teachers to examine the issue and know that they are more needed now than ever before.

While a digital culture seems to be panicked and creates a sense of distrust, and even hate, toward those in our past, these children, being exposed to that distrust and panic, may not be as motivated to move toward a healthy development of moral reasoning when exposed to those exceptional moral exemplars. The cultural drumbeat doesn't allow that. It drowns out the good that these exceptional moral exemplars did while here. However, rather than trying to cut down those jungles, we should be irrigating deserts.

The research shows that we are in need of attainable and relevant exemplars. Students are motivated when they are personally engaged with those relevant exemplars and that engagement moves them further in their own personal moral development.[5]

However, in a digital world, who should these relevant and attainable moral exemplars be? The digital world may offer many. But let's do the math. They need attainable and relevant moral exemplars. These models of morality should be accessible. And every day that door closes in millions of rooms across our country. Sadly, the intentional educator preparation programs and intellectual research may be ignoring our best opportunity.

Who would be best suited to be those attainable and relevant exemplars now, especially in a digital world? Shepherd heart teachers. Rather than being just a guide on the side, a facilitator that boots up the technology and gets out of the way, teachers are our best hope to be moral exemplars that students engage with on a daily basis. Rather than the old standard of just reading the biography to the class and listing the moral attributes of the hero in the story, shepherd heart teachers can be the heroes themselves.

Students want moral exemplars to be relevant to their lives. Shepherd heart teachers are those life changers and they can create a moral center that students will emulate and respect. We know that learning happens when you have engaged teachers with motivated learners. Motivation is created when those teachers are moral examples for students.

While the culture may have us believe that the exceptional moral exemplars of the past, because they may not be as relevant or attainable now, are no longer needed, that isn't true. Exceptional moral exemplars have always been exceptional. And they don't stop being exceptional just because the culture calls them irrelevant or unattainable. The problem is that culture wants to ignore those exemplars or vilify them in some way.

And because the digital generation lives in a culturally loud world of posts and tweets, these children can be affected and their feelings or beliefs about the exceptional moral exemplar may change, be negatively affected, or have no effect at all. That doesn't stop the exceptional moral exemplar from being the exemplar. But we cannot ignore the research.

Doing so is trying to cut down the jungle. While we should continue presenting those exceptional moral exemplars, we should irrigate the deserts and present the relevant moral exemplar as well. And that's the teacher.

THE RESPONSIBILITIES WE HAVE

We have a dual role in education. While there are countless items on our list as teachers and administrators, at the end, we should hand these children and adolescents off to their adult life with two things.

First, they should have the information and knowledge to be successful and participate in life, whatever pursuit they choose. Some will go to college and some will go to careers. And they create their lives, hopefully lives made better because of the knowledge they learned from us.

But the second element of our role as educators is that, while they were with us, we passed down wisdom and morality to these learners. How can we best do that? While it may be systematic and busy to organize the knowledge aspect of our classrooms, the elements of wisdom and morality will take a focus on three primary approaches to our work.

Transferring

Children pick up on everything. And we carry that through adolescence. In fact, modeling after those things we see in others never really goes away. If we, as educators, are best to instill wisdom in those we teach, we can do that by intentionally practicing the elements of wisdom and morality when we work with them.

And if we intentionally practice those things, we must actually be that person. The hope is that we, along with the passion to change lives, will be wise and moral as we teach children. Again, shepherd heart teachers typically represent these elements anyway. But they need to be encouraged to exhibit these intentionally.

That's transference. That's handing off these same things to children. We should not just be managers of their time while they gather information and gain knowledge while with us. They should become better people because of who we are. That's transference of the best from one generation to the next.

Engagement

We are in the same room together with learners. But are we truly with them? In group settings, some people just naturally engage with the teacher. And because the job can be incredibly busy at times, we tend to let those who engage with us become those we engage with most. We have to flip that around.

In the digital world, we have to take the initiative to move beyond those who are the easiest and engage with every learner. We can change lives. But we need to change every life. Shepherd hearts can do this because it's why they most likely chose this profession in the first place. But in the digital world, this becomes even more important.

Remember that some will give you the wrong definition of facilitate and may attempt to minimize your role. That's when you need to not allow yourself to be pushed to the side. You have to engage. Intentionally engage with every kid.

Shepherding

We arrive back to the concept, a paradigm really, of shepherding. It's never easy to take responsibility for other people's children. So many minds, personalities, and attitudes, all thrown together under your watch. However, that's where the shepherd works best, in knowing how to draw the best out of each learner.

They need to be cared for while with us. That means we don't just give them information to gain knowledge. We give them ourselves. They need a shepherd.

If we can transfer wisdom and morality to our learners, if we can engage with every learner every day, and if we can take on the responsibility of being shepherds for them, they will be able to function much better when their entire adult world is affected by a digital culture in the future.

THE HOPE WE HAVE

If we see this new opportunity of the emerging digital environments in education as our best to also transfer wisdom and morality and engage students as never before, there are immeasurable things we can hope for when we are gone. One of the best ways to do our work is to do those things that we know live on after we are gone.

To work today for things that will be better forty years after you're gone is a great way to work, and that should be one of our major goals in the classroom. We should ask ourselves the question, "Will the future family of this learner have a better life because I taught their parent or grandparent?" If that's the way we teach, what might we hope for?

THE DANGERS WE FACE

So should we allow ourselves, as shepherd heart teachers, to be replaced or relegated to a nonessential role in a technology-rich educational environment, what could we possibly face in our future? The consequences could be many but we will focus on only two.

1. The future adult generations could be in a world that is controlled so much by a vulnerable digital system that every aspect of life is connected, and subject to, that vulnerability. If we have not transferred our wisdom, if we have allowed ourselves to be taken out of the learning equation, or if we have not placed wisdom and morality as foundations for those generations while they are with us, they will have to navigate that world without some important elements for success and well-being.

    That world could be consumed with social media pressures and reactionary postings that are always given credibility and considered believable. If they have not learned discernment, they will tolerate and/or believe everything.

    They will be in an anxiety-ridden world that sways dramatically from one end to the next almost daily. And they will have to respond accordingly. But they can't do that effectively if they have not been fully immersed in wisdom and morality while in school.
2. The generations just beyond the current generations will lose these elements altogether. It will be difficult or impossible to recapture any moral cultures we may have lost by that time. We will lose that base of wisdom in our classrooms, all for the sake of technology and tolerance.

We don't have to lose anything. Shepherd heart teachers fill our classrooms now. They know the imperative of engaging with generations of learners. They know they can do so now more than ever. We need to create those learning systems to empower teachers to engage with empowered students.

NOTES

1. The NCES Fast Facts Tool provides quick answers to many education questions. National Center for Education Statistics, n.d., https://nces.ed.gov/fastfacts/display.asp?id=372.

2. C. S. Lewis, *The Abolition of Man; or, Reflections on Education with Special Reference to the Teaching of English in the Upper Forms of Schools* (New York: Macmillan Company, 1947).

3. L. Kohlberg, "Education, Moral Development and Faith," *Journal of Moral Education* 4, no. 1 (1974): 5–16, doi:10.1080/0305724740040102.

4. H. Han, J. Kim, C. Jeong, and G. L. Cohen, "Attainable and Relevant Moral Exemplars Are More Effective Than Extraordinary Exemplars in Promoting Voluntary Service Engagement," *Frontiers in Psychology* 8, no. 283 (2017), http://doi.org/10.3389/fpsyg.2017.00283.

5. H. Malin, P. J. Ballard, and W. Damon, "Civic Purpose: An Integrated Construct for Understanding Civic Development in Adolescence," *Human Development* 58, no. 2 (2015): 103–30, doi:http://dx.doi.org.ezproxy.liberty.edu/10.1159/000381655.

4

THE SILHOUETTE

Belief Systems of Shepherd Heart Educators

We don't talk much about morality in our classrooms. While this was a common foundation in education for centuries, not much is said about morality in K–12 schools now. Some might say we have character education but what may serve as character education typically depends on the cultural and political correctness of the day.

A moral center, an understood common morality doesn't seem to have a place in our curriculum or classrooms. In a culture that has convinced educators that they could be criminalized by invoking any statements that would betray a separation of church and state, teachers are afraid to utter a word about anything connected to their moral belief systems.

Government was never meant to prevent religion nor was it meant to promote one. Government is meant to protect religion. Our founding fathers believed that we have certain and particular rights that have been endowed by God and that the government they were creating was meant to protect those rights.

The most damaging element of our modern approach is that we take the moral basis of our most connected, and most passionate, life changers (our teachers) and we silence them from sharing that moral basis. We scare our teachers into believing they must leave their belief systems at home when they leave for the campus.

If we are sincere in our belief systems, and if they inform us in how we interact with those around us, we must also know that they inform us in how we engage with learners. With agendas in a social media–driven world that constantly post something other than teaching the goodness of moral and virtuous living, we need shepherd heart teachers to engage students through their internal belief systems and worldview in the classroom.

So let's be clear. No one advocates any establishment of religion forced on a population by a government. The creators of the documents that founded this nation were responding to this practice and knew it had serious consequences when government entities organized, legislated, and demanded allegiance to any particular religion. You can find those references consistently throughout the founding documents.

However, these men were not advocating an absence or elimination of religion from a person's journey through life. It was a personal matter but it was not a secret or shameful matter. Some of these men were deeply religious and some were not. But there were references to an external moral code constantly mentioned and voiced by these men. They wanted to protect religion and they didn't want the government forcing religion by law.

So the shepherd heart teacher isn't a lawbreaker for possessing a profound adherence to a belief system. And that belief system alone, if it has virtuous responsibility toward others in it, informs the teacher that forcing their own religious beliefs on children is wrong.

The shepherd heart teacher won't try to proselytize children in classrooms but will bring to the classroom the best qualities of their belief system. It's not about converting children but about being who you are when you engage with children. We should encourage that.

Yet educators sometimes may feel that they should compartmentalize their lives because they work in an industry that doesn't want their beliefs to affect their work. A shepherd heart teacher doesn't want to push their religion but one must be free to exercise an adherence to a moral code, especially when working with learners.

We cannot establish religion but we can establish morality in our classrooms. We don't have to voice our religious preferences but we can allow our internal moral voice to teach us more about loving children, engaging with them, and seeing them as deeply in need of wisdom and moral models.

Bringing their belief systems into their engagement with students is not an epic matter. It is a matter, however, of tapping into the wisdom that can be shared from the adult to the child. That wisdom, at least in shepherd heart teachers, stems from their belief systems.

While shepherd heart teachers have strong and solid belief systems, they may believe they must hide those or keep those only in their head and heart while working with children. Why would we take the central driving element of a shepherd heart teacher and erase it from their work?

THE DEFINITIVE SHEPHERD HEART

Children, for the most part, spend a tremendous amount of time with adults other than their parents. Teachers interact with students five days a week and these interactions help shape the child's thinking about the world. Though we might believe that children come to us "as is," it's important to know that a child is always gathering information, processing that information through current filters, and molding that information to fit their understanding of their environment. And as they mature, the filters may change.

What we say and what we do affects children. They are constantly defining, redefining, and trying to make sense of the world and how they fit in that world. Our words, our actions, and our engagement with students will have significant effects. So it's important that we, as teachers, engage properly and appropriately with the learners sitting in our classrooms.

As adults, we may have already fashioned our belief systems. We may feel we already know our world, know where we fit, and know how it all works. It's important, if we work with generations of children growing up in a world they will eventually lead, to instill in them a sense of that world and how it works. It's crucial that we think beyond ourselves. The point is that we, as educators, must have a personal belief system, a sense of our worldview that informs us, anchors us, and instills in us a genuine sense of shepherding.

Now, any time "belief systems" are discussed, the focus is primarily on the two words. "Belief" implies religious adherence. Or maybe it implies political preference—fundamental, conservative, liberal. The word "belief" carries with it certain connotations.

The word "systems" can be just as difficult, bringing with it the idea that it's a systemic foundation that defines, describes, and dictates to the individual all that they do or feel.

However, when we discuss belief systems for the educator, it goes beyond a simple definition. The educator must be one who has a belief system that tells him or her why he or she is doing what he or she does. It's a sense of responsibility. It's an understanding of the role of the adult in the classroom who, when the door closes, can be trusted to shepherd children.

There are, however, some elements of a belief system that should be present. There is a significant crucial foundation for anyone who might lead children. And as said previously, while there are many in education, we specifically point only to the shepherd heart teacher for the following. It's important to be reminded that, rather than speaking against anyone or anything, we are speaking for something.

An educator informed by a genuine belief system will be known as one who believes in a moral code that has been created outside one's self. We have a moral code to teach children and that moral code is not affected by someone's subjective opinion or popular culture.

An educator who has a belief system in a moral code created beyond one's self has a personal adherence to guiding principles developed externally and not subject to his or her own, or the community's, opinion. This educator has an understanding of how this moral code develops the child and gives the child a solid foundation. An educator informed by his or her belief systems does not leave those belief systems at home when he or she reports to work.

Specifically, belief systems for the shepherd heart educator are:

- *An adherence to a moral code.*
- *That moral code has been created externally rather than by the individual alone.*
- *The moral code is defined by elements of truth, goodness, and beauty, always seeking the good of, and for, others.*
- *The educator is led by these elements personally and the moral code is not employed as a proselytizing agent but, rather, informs the practice and engagement of the educator to the student.*

Some would say that they would not want someone of a different faith teaching their child. The fear is that the teacher would try to indoctrinate their child in the particular, and different, religion. Some parent might shudder at the idea that someone of a different faith might be teaching his or her child, but the truth is that, if the teacher is informed and led by a moral code created externally, that should be preferred over having no moral code at all.

This is not an indictment on anyone's particular religious or political preference. It's known that the genesis documents forming our nation were created by men who may or may not have been particularly religious in practice but did understand that there is a moral code. Our nation was not founded on an absence of morality in the classroom, but rather on an absence of the government forcing particular religious adherence to any one religion.

An educator informed by his or her belief system will systemically practice the goodness of that belief system. It's what the educator looks to for his or her own personal efficacy and passionate approach to the classroom.

The essence of the moral code is good and goodness. The moral code cares for man and embodies truth and virtuous elements of truth. The moral code is spiritual and speaks into the spirit of man.

A shepherd heart teacher will be guided by this moral code. And that teacher is connected to this moral center that informs him or her daily. That connection will be the driving force behind his or her action and his or her practice as he or she engages with digital learners. Because the digital learner is faced with so many opinions, now and even more in the future, the shepherd heart teacher will consistently bring the learner back to the moral center.

When the latest posts stir anxiety or create chaos, the shepherd heart teacher will focus the learner on the elements of truth and goodness from that moral code. Rather than depending on the confusion caused by a world of anxious tweets, the shepherd heart teacher will ground the student in a moral code that can be relied on to build true character.

So in a private education environment, adherence to specific and particular worldviews can be expected. Anyone educating learners in these environments should be expected to be directly connected to those particular beliefs. For instance, a religious university would expect those who teach us to be loyal to a religious worldview.

In the public education world, though, because our culture tethers morality to religion, the person who strictly adheres to a religious belief is often seen as being unable to practice his or her belief system without being religiously motivated. But again, we are not expecting a religious practice here.

The concept is of moral education with an undisputed understanding that morality in the classroom was not questioned in our nation before nor should it be now. There are absolutes and objective truths and we need shepherd heart teachers to not be pressured to teach that these no longer exist. Nor should we leave these moral foundations in a vacuumed room, closed to the learner who is left with the idea that there is no right or wrong and all life is subjective and shifting.

We can, and should, expect educators to be led by a belief system. And we should expect educators to have that informed by a moral center initiating from a moral code. We should support their efforts to change the lives of children because of their sense of calling to the classroom.

The purpose of the church/state issue was not meant to cleanse the classroom of the moral code. It's meant to protect both entities. *We will not bode well if freedom of religion is not protected by the state and we will not bode well if the state loses the protection of a population of shepherd heart teachers with a strong adherence to a moral code.*

If we remove the shepherd heart teacher, we lose the foundation and the anchor in our future classrooms. The true aspects of a moral code will dictate a respect for government and authority. This is true in the genuine and pure beliefs created by the moral code. The state has nothing to fear in a population of shepherd heart teachers. While agreeing that the teacher has allegiance to the moral code, that code teaches obedience to government and authority.

These shepherd heart teachers support authority and will teach children to do so as well. Yes, they will teach children to be discerning and they will teach children that the digital world can be dangerous. And they will teach the good and the virtuous thing. Rather than proselyting children, they will teach children that there is a right and wrong and that there are objective absolutes and truths. Any government will thrive with a population of leaders taught thusly, even if the internet goes down.

Belief systems are a significant part of life. And the moral code does not exist simply within ourselves. A moral code has always recognized the common good of society, an understanding that the community is composed of individuals and those individuals have a "common good" that is shared and lays a foundation for how we behave toward each other. In a digital world, though, social media can give the appearance of always speaking for the community but may not feel any obligation toward the common good. And digital generations are presented with ideas that would remove objective truth and a moral code.

Morality is not just about doing the right thing. It's about doing the good thing, not something only for yourself but for others first. Shepherd heart teachers instinctively know to do that. Their belief systems consistently lead them to do that. They should be encouraged to pass that on to the next generations.

Our greatest hope in the future will be leaders who have belief systems and wisdom and are transferring those to their next generations. Rather than being afraid of their belief systems in their classrooms, shepherd heart teachers today have to reinforce those things now. Our future, in many ways, depends on it.

THE SILHOUETTE OF THE SHEPHERD HEART

So how is this done? How can we teach and train teachers to exercise and practice their belief systems in public schools without being misunderstood? How do we help them know that their belief systems can inform their practice and engagement with learners?

Remember that the belief systems and the moral code of shepherd heart teachers are not proselytizing agents. Public schools are not churches or political assemblies. They are gathering places for the children of a community, and these gathering places should be filled with passionate adults wanting to improve lives for the better. Transferring wisdom and morality, while also giving them the necessary content learning, is key to these generations.

But how can we do that in a culture that seems to want teachers to leave those belief systems at home? And conversely, how can we encourage teachers to bring their belief systems with them in a trusted manner? What kind of picture would we draw for these teachers that they might be able to shape their engagement correctly?

Being a shepherd heart teacher who is informed by personal and moral belief systems can be compared to a silhouette. The definition of silhouette is "an image outlined against a light background." As we engage students, we are in direct connection with them. We act, speak, and listen directly. We engage. And how we engage will affect them directly as well. We should project a profile of the silhouette.

The silhouette is not a shadow. A shadow prevents light. A silhouette is a profile that is clearly seen *because* of the light. The lighter background of a shepherd heart teacher is the belief system of that teacher. And that profile is sharp and distinct because of that background.

Shepherd heart teachers are not judgmental nor are they proselyting learners. They are silhouettes, their moral profile distinct against that lighter background of their belief systems.

When we enter our classrooms, we must remain ethical and teach with integrity. Our belief systems tell us that. We should not judge or measure the value of kids. They are all valuable. Our belief systems tell us that.

The silhouette. The profile of the shepherd heart teacher. Transferring wisdom and centering their innovative and transformed classrooms on a moral center that protects timeless truth and hands off that generation to their adult lives, prepared and better off.

5

THE DISTINCTION OF MORALITY IN EDUCATION

Morality: "Principles concerning the distinction between right and wrong or good and bad behavior."
Character: "One or more attributes that make up and distinguish an individual."

Education has always played a major role in shaping culture. Thomas Jefferson and the founding fathers had, as a guiding force, a nation of good citizens in mind when addressing the creation of schools in our country. But just as important was the recognition of the principles outlined and articulated in the documents from that time period. While the individual, the citizen, is important, it's the moral agreements, the principles that form the foundation, that are most important. For years, the school was a place where one learned those principles. We learned respect, honor, and integrity.

For more than a hundred years, we have been on an escalator of change in how we move children through childhood. And the greatest dynamic shift can be seen in the distinctions of character and morality. More specifically, how we teach character and morality. Somewhere we flipped the order.

Whereas we had always focused on the moral agreements and principles, we started shifting the focus to the individual and character. We never hear of moral education. Rather, we hear of character education.

We teach students to adhere to their characters, teach students to rely and depend on their inner selves, and try to help them develop those inner selves. The fundamental issue with character education is when we redefine and modify good traits using only current culture as the watermark.

We remove the foundation when we do not focus on the moral code, the principles. It began when we started focusing on self-esteem in the classroom. We started teaching students to question everything. We started teaching value-driven concepts rather than principle-driven concepts. We removed any idea of absolute truth, objective truth.

But we've always had, in education, a moral code, a moral center, that informed us and held us to a set of guiding principles. Those common understandings are important.

No one in a classroom should want a child to feel unworthy. We should want that child to feel worthy and to feel that he or she has value. However, in focusing on self-esteem development, particularly if we focus on self-worth with no moral center, we teach the child to look to him- or herself for the answers.

No one is perfect and no one has all the answers. While it's easy to accept this with a group of elementary school children, those children eventually grow to be adults. If we spend our time patting them on the head and making them believe that their rightness is all that matters, that doesn't play well when they are grown. Goodness is more important than rightness.

Teaching the individual that the individual is most important absent the moral code leaves the individual relying on his or her own feelings to determine how he or she operates in a culture. And in a world driven by social media, the individual can become addicted to trusting the untrustworthy posts of anyone with an account or device and can spell close enough that autocorrect can fix it.

Not everything we think is totally accurate. Not everything we do is totally good. We are flawed creatures prone to mistakes. Self-esteem is a good thing when it teaches confidence and independence. However, it's bad when it breeds arrogance and isolated selfishness.

Teaching values and choices absent moral teaching raises the individual above all others. This limits the child's world and creates a bubble that surrounds the child in which the child is always good and always right.

If we teach young children that all they think is good and they are the chooser of good action, then inject them into a values-driven environment charged with social media pressure, the generation will be self-centered.

Each individual will look to whatever information he or she can find and there will be plenty out there. And that information will have already determined the correct choice and will force adherence to that correct choice or face the penalty of the community.

Raising the individual above a set of principles removes the foundation necessary for character development. The moral center and understandings of a nation are left to drift in a society so influenced by social media that the latest postings and rants created by many, who care not about the genuine character development of these generations, can become mistaken for truth or, at the very least, options for truth.

A vacuum is created when we teach children there is no objective truth. If we place children in a daily environment in which they are taught that no absolute truth exists beyond the individual, and each individual operates within his or her own personal truth, these children can become slaves to the latest and loudest opinions and reactions published in a digital world. If we have not taught these children discernment or grounded these children on a moral center, we leave them untethered from any anchor.

Character education, as it stands today, cannot fill that vacuum.

There's a possibility that morality is never mentioned in classrooms in a digital world because it sounds religious and we fear religion if it's in the context of education. Religion tied to education is reserved for those wealthy enough to afford private school.

It can sound political. In a digital world, where nothing escapes politics, the intrusion of countless posts in a student's world can define morality as fundamental conservatism or open-minded liberalism.

Yet morality isn't political or religious. Rather, it's a set of guiding principles in a community. Teaching through a moral lens can be difficult to navigate in a digital world, but that doesn't mean it can't be done.

EXAMINING THE PIECES

When addressing morality and character, we can look closely at the pieces that play into our current state in education.

First, self-esteem. The greatest thing a shepherd heart teacher can do is create relationships with students that give them an intrinsic sense of self-worth. Knowing ourselves and being comfortable with who we are is significant and important for anyone. Hopefully, the home is the center of that for the child.

But even in those instances in which it's not, shepherd heart teachers have the opportunity to create within the child something that stays with them throughout their lives, something that tells them they have value.

However, so much focus can be placed on this that it goes beyond a healthy development. In an effort to make children feel good about themselves, we can become nothing more than simple pats on the head. Children have the capacity to understand that they can be wrong. They have the ability to know they are not the center of the universe. We cannot become guilty of teaching children that they are so good that their goodness overarches everything they experience.

Self-esteem is focused on the self. Rather than instilling a sense of responsibility for others, self-centered focus can remove any obligation the child should have for anyone beyond themselves. In those early years, children must know how to exist in a world that doesn't embrace the idea that everything revolves around them.

If we have generations of adults in our future who cannot see beyond themselves, we will become more isolated. The digital world boasts of connections and community. Yet digital connections are not community and don't necessarily claim a loyalty to a common good. Even in a world in which posts are frequent, these can be random at best and isolated reactions meant to stir up and incite at worst.

In a self-esteem-driven world, propagated and directed by digital means, everyone is right and everyone can demand attention. Shepherd heart teachers can ensure we balance how we teach self-esteem. It's never in a vacuum.

Second, the concept of questioning everything. It seems that we created a scenario for children years ago that included cynicism, skepticism, and rebellion. It's almost as if there is an American script for children that demands that, once they reach their teenage years, they should rebel.

Many often point to the mid-part of the last century as the model for genuine teenage development. Those generations who rebelled, particularly against their parents, were seen as true examples of adolescence in our country. Not only should you rebel, it became accepted as the rite of passage. You must rebel or you're not normal.

And the first step to rebellion is to place within the young child a sense of obligation to that script, that cynical mistrust of anyone in authority, and that typically starts closest to home then radiates out. So question your parents first.

Now, no parent is perfect. In fact, parenthood is difficult to manage well even in the best scenario. But it's not the job of the educator to facilitate, support, or create rebellion within children toward parents. And it's not the job of education to gather children behind closed doors and foster a cynical, contemptuous nature within a child.

We most assuredly need to be discerning in our lives. Adults must consistently weigh everything. And discernment has to be taught. But it's not taught by creating a "first response" reaction to authority that is questioning, cynical, and rebellious.

Take a child who has grown up in a self-esteem environment in classrooms, add a cynical rebellious attitude within that child, layer onto that a digital world consumed with overwhelming posts unsubstantiated and harmful, and you have a generation of adults in our future with no concept of a moral center.

Third, values-driven character education. While it's important to develop the various elements of character in children, doing so without a moral code leaves the child looking to something else for direction.

If that something else is the individual, the self, and if that self is driven to a cynical questioning of everything, and if everyone and anyone can influence the community and culture with a simple post, values become nothing more than immediate choices that serve the self at the moment. And this causes reactions and anxiety. It's difficult to teach children values unless we have something for them to value.

Lastly, removing absolute and objective truth. Moral education is anchored in a moral truth and an appreciation of the beauty and the goodness of that truth. In our effort to sweep any reference to religion and politics out the door, we also remove any trace of absolute truth.

Doubt becomes uncertainty and uncertainty becomes an aimless wandering through a future culture. And while it may not seem to be too damaging when we only look at a room full of children, it becomes much more serious when it's an entire community of adults. It's the generations that matter and that's why we must have shepherd heart teachers.

William Bennet, secretary of education from 1985 to 1988, wrote extensively about virtue and morality and the significance of presenting moral examples in classrooms and on campuses, stating that children would take morality seriously if those teaching them would serve as examples. He states about children that "with their own eyes they must see adults take morality seriously."[1]

Lawrence Kohlberg spoke of the "hidden curriculum" in education.[2] This is the idea that the moral examples of those in authority can create a foundation on a campus that informs and affects the school community. Student behavior can be affected by educator practice.

While it may be true that we don't discuss morality on our campuses much and we may not be talking about it in our training programs, that doesn't mean that our responsibility to create a morally centered classroom is no longer relevant or needed. As adults, we have to shoulder the responsibility to teach wisdom and practice the best qualities of morality in our engagement with students.

It seems to be that many believe that any mention of morality in our classrooms belongs only in private schools connected to a religious foundation or purpose. In other words, if the parent wants their child in an environment infused with moral adults who live and speak morality intentionally as part of the school culture, they should pay for it (beyond the school taxes they already pay) and separate their child from the mainstream. But that's not the way it once was in this country. Any parent could expect that in any classroom in the not too distant past.

We've focused on college preparation and career readiness. We fund food programs and social services. We increase the technology with our kids. None of that's bad or wrong.

But we fear focusing on morality because we don't know how to handle it, train it, teach it, or talk about it. It may be because we think it's better to just not venture into that territory because we are then left to question whose morality, what's the definition of it, and how do we control it? Or maybe we just don't know how to measure it. Or it may be that we just don't see the need.

In 1954, Martin Luther King Jr., a young preacher one year away from his doctorate, spoke at Second Baptist Church in Detroit, Michigan.[3] His message that day was one of the most powerful sermons ever preached on the moral foundations of our nation. His words were relevant then and they are relevant now.

He eloquently spoke of the foundations and the values we were beginning to abandon in our country. His call for those gathered that day, and we can apply those same words to us today, was to rediscover and recover these significant things.

Dr. King left no doubt to his listeners that there are unchanging and absolute moral principles and laws in this world, "just as abiding as the physical laws."[4]

If we follow what he articulated that morning, we understand that physical laws aren't questioned. But his words remain true even today that, just as those physical laws aren't questioned, neither should we ignore the moral foundations and laws of this world. Objective truth and an unquestioned moral code. A duty to acknowledge that objective truth and moral code. Can we rediscover that?

One day in our future, they may look around and wonder, where did we first embrace the idea that every person must think only of him- or herself, even at the expense of any other? When did we throw out any idea or allegiance to an absolute truth that guides us, leaving us to the whims and posts of others who may or may not be trustworthy?

When did we start becoming so cynical and rebellious to any in authority, making it almost impossible for them to do their job? And when did we become nothing more than isolated pieces of a disconnected community that looks only to bandwidth to define itself as connected and unified?

They may find that it started in classrooms.

Some would take that and, as typical, use it as an indictment against teachers. We should flip that, though, and use it as an encouragement for teachers. Outside the home, no individual stands better positioned to engage and influence generations of children who will one day lead us. And the shepherd heart teacher in a digital world has more time for that engagement. Shepherd heart teachers transfer wisdom grounded in truth, goodness and beauty.

NOTES

1. W. J. Bennett, *The Book of Virtues for Young People: A Treasury of Great Moral Stories* (New York: Simon and Schuster, 1997).

2. W. M. Kurtines and J. L. Gewirtz, *Handbook of Moral Behavior and Development Application* (Hillsdale, NJ: L. Erlbaum Associates, 1991).

3. M. L. King, C. Carson, S. Carson, S. Englander, T. Jackson, and G. L. Smith, *The Papers of Martin Luther King, Jr.* (Berkeley, CA: University of California Press, 2007).

4. M. L. King, C. Carson, and P. Holloran, *A Knock at Midnight: Inspiration from the Great Sermons of Reverend Martin Luther King, Jr.* (New York: Intellectual Properties Management in Association with Warner Books, 2000).

6

POINTS OF WISDOM AND THE CURRICULUM OF THE SHEPHERD

POINTS OF WISDOM

Conscientious engagement with students from shepherd heart teachers ensures that our next generations of leaders have a solid foundation in the moral principles and historical understanding that have characterized our nation from its beginning. While knowing that we haven't always been perfect and sometimes have made serious errors in our judgment, we have several points of wisdom that have defined us as people committed to a peaceful and just society.

Shepherd heart teachers have the opportunity to embody these points of wisdom in the classroom, instill these in our children, and transfer these in a way that keeps them engrained in our national community.

While there are many of these points of wisdom, there are particular elements that must be part of this transfer of wisdom. We will only address two but these are responses to the direction we are headed and the cultural shifts our digital generations face.

These two anchors of our communities could become relics of a past that future generations only learn about in their studies about that past if we don't engage intentionally with our children in classrooms and on campuses. Again, there are certainly more but these two are primary for our digital learners.

A PROFOUND REGARD FOR HUMAN LIFE

A fundamental anchor in morality, engrained in all of mankind, is a deep, profound regard for human life.

Regard for human life is an anchor. And if we are to transfer wisdom to digital generations who will one day lead us, we must promote, support, and teach students that this anchor remains significant. There is no need to quote statistics, rally forces, or debate our arguments. Human life, in and of itself, is to be considered a nonnegotiable standard. That is at risk when we don't teach it.

Establishing truth, goodness, and beauty in children instills a regard for human life that is profound. Transferring wisdom and morality to generations requires we teach children to have the highest regard for human life itself. And we cannot ignore or abandon this requirement for our generations.

To begin, any discussion about a regard for human life seems to always demand a debate lost in political arenas, morphing into a "rights" issue of what individuals are allowed to do related to abortion. And that then morphs into a debate based on personal views founded on spiritual beliefs of what an individual passionately feels should and shouldn't be done. It gets lost in the confusion, tied to an entire set of value systems and acceptable practices. It's difficult to separate it from emotional responses.

But a profound regard for human life is being chipped away in many areas of the digital world. The four primary areas where this regard is ignored are wars (almost treated as daily threats to life and a peaceful existence), crime (murder, terrorism where life is destroyed meaninglessly), executions, and abortion. These end life. And ending life in any manner threatens to diminish the profound regard we must have for human life. While understanding that difficult decisions may face us at times, we cannot lose a profound regard for human life and become careless in how we see the sacredness of it.

The danger is that these generations of children are being exposed to it sooner. In the digital world, the exposure rate increases the danger that these children will never develop that profound regard for human life, that precious understanding that life is to be honored and protected. Even video games remind students that life is not worth much. In 40 years, what will these current generations face in a world that has abandoned a profound regard for human life?

To be clear, this isn't an argument against anyone or anything. This is a plea to teach *for* something: a profound regard for human life. No matter where one stands on any related issues, surely we can agree that teaching children to have a profound regard for human life is a good and virtuous thing. Instilling that, talking about it, being intentional about it, with children is important. Rather than focusing on an act, we focus on the moral foundation of that profound regard.

We are talking about classrooms and children. Educators as shepherd heart teachers. As generations of our learners sit in our classrooms each day, we must teach wisdom. And wisdom, with a moral center inherent in all people, knows that regard for human life means regard for human life.

Related to the primary areas we've listed, any time we lose that profound regard for human life, we see a diminished value placed on others. In our own country, we have seen what can occur when that profound regard for human life, that diminished value placed on others, is ignored. Whether it be removing people forcefully from their native lands, enslaving and brutalizing others for personal gain or discriminating against others simply because they are different, we find that there is a disregard for human life and the value of others.

Should we teach that we only look to legal rights to shape our beliefs, we could become keepers of a possible moral vacuum within us that waits to be told how we feel and what we can do. Yet, there is a robust moral center within us all, an intrinsic sense of right and wrong ingrained in each individual. Wisdom doesn't look to permissible and acceptable practice within the culture to shape or reshape that center.

Having a profound regard for human life starts with children. Though children will most naturally lean toward bad behavior, we teach them to practice good behavior. While there is a legitimate moral center, a sense of right and wrong, we still have to shepherd children to look to that moral center for guidance.

And the moral center doesn't change to accommodate the cultural shifts and political wishes of society. We know that life is sacred. That's why we celebrate it.

Personal freedoms that exponentially expand to become political rights don't change the fact that human life is sacred. If we do not shepherd children to understand that, no matter the protests, politics, or public thinking, life is sacred, we will experience a profound loss of that moral belief once they are our leaders.

So many want to focus on the pinpoint "when does human life begin" question. Science often seems to have a variety of responses to the question. And there does seem to be an authoritative agreement that human life begins before the delivery room. In fact, there is evidence that human life has begun and has been evident long before the delivery room.[1] But, it's not the beginning of life we are addressing here. It's the ending of life.

If we are shepherd heart teachers transferring wisdom to generations, it's not the technical matter of when human life begins that is our focus. It's the matter of ending human life at all, for any reason, that lives within the moral center. Ending any human life, at whatever stage, is crossing a line.

In the four primary areas, we have to remain committed to the truth that ending life diminishes all of us. And we should not focus solely on any one of those areas. We should focus on the whole of it. Decisions are made and actions are taken but we cannot afford to lose our profound regard for human life. It's often too easy to reduce any argument about "human life" issues to abortion only. But it's not that alone. The value of human life can be threatened in all areas of life if we lose a profound regard for it.

We have a tendency to show contempt, disrespect, and ill will toward others. And children practice this quite naturally. But if we lose the opportunity to establish within our generations that life is honored above all other engagements between people, it becomes much easier to cross the line once they are adults.

A disregard for the significant, profound essence of a human life gives freedom to treat the ending of lives casually. It becomes easier because of the cultural acceptance. Rather than holding anyone in contempt about their own personal feelings about the issue, this is an admonition to educators that we must not abandon the tremendous responsibility to ground our children in the truth that human life is precious. When we engage with our children, we must teach wisdom, and wisdom rests in a profound regard for human life.

A PROFOUND RESPECT FOR THE HISTORICAL NATIONAL NARRATIVE

Children learn about the establishment of our country and how those brave men and women who created this model of freedom took great risks to do so. However, this was an experiment. It's difficult for people to handle imminent freedom. But those individuals who created this experiment were willing to establish freedom as our primary foundation.

Freedom is not guaranteed for any person or country. While this freedom is an expected part of life in our nation, that doesn't mean it's experienced like this everywhere and it doesn't mean that it's always going to be available. Living in a society that protects freedom is important.

In a large population of countless numbers of people, there are just as many ideas and opinions. Those opinions and ideas may or may not be good for children. While our children are young and forming their perceptions and personalities, what we present to them, what we show them, and what we teach them is crucial.

In former generations, we could rest in the fact that, even though there were many ideas and opinions out there, we didn't particularly feel threatened that those would touch our children because there wasn't a way to get to them.

We depended on our child's teacher to be a moral person and an educated professional. We relied on those who were with our children during sports activities and extracurricular events. We trusted they would be good people doing good things with our most precious treasure.

And we knew the opinions and ideas that we never wanted our children to be exposed to were out there. We live in a country in which we exercise freedom. That freedom is not a byword for us. It's not a casual or careless quality of our national life. It's the very foundation on which we thrive.

So even though we knew ideas and opinions that might not be beneficial for our children, we vigorously protected the rights of those who would have them. We just didn't want those ideas and opinions thrust on our children. Free to have that idea or opinion, not free to teach it to my child.

The buffer that gave us peace about this was that, though we knew those things were out there, they existed only in the living rooms of those who possessed them. Everybody has the right to their opinion, as long as they keep it in their living room.

The world changed with the automobile. The highway is where everything is brought out of the living room and mixes together in one happy mess. People live together in relative peace, even people with radically different ideas and opinions. As long as everyone keeps it to their own living room. But the highway pulls it all out of the living room and clashes it together.

In any typical day, the emotions, fears, anxieties, ideas, and opinions come together out there. It seems that everyone is carrying out their own personal drama in their own personal vehicle. And we somehow have to navigate our way to and from our destination. And we need to get along and be nice. It usually works. Until it doesn't. And our culture, our ideas, and our opinions crash together.

That, though, is only a precursor to the world faced by digital generations. And just as the concrete highway changed this world, what we referred to in the beginning as the information superhighway did much the same. Except it's not vehicles and cars. It's information. It's opinions. It's ideas. It's things that help and things that hurt.

It was called an information superhighway for a reason. The ideas and the opinions were now capable of being launched outside the living rooms and placed at the fingertips of anyone with a computer. And in the digital world, these young generations have access to all this information.

It's no longer safe to just rely on the one person who might be around our child during the day. Our child may be exposed to many people throughout the day. How? Through the internet. One might just think that this is an outdated, irrelevant thought that does not have the credibility to consider. It's not. What we present to our children affects them. What we introduce to our children will change them. What we example before our children will play into what they perceive about their world.

And just as the highway changed the world many years ago, the internet changed the world. However, this isn't just an incremental change that slowly behaves and doesn't interrupt, disrupt, or disturb a culture.

This is an incredibly exponential change, one that demands and forces. Though we might still remain somewhat in charge of how much of this change pushes into our life, our children may not have that same ability. The world, as each innovation increases in its deployment, is tethering those innovations to required and necessary components of normal life.

Our children, in forty years, may not have the choices we have to engage with it or not.

Even now the commonality of digital technology has pushed everything out of the living rooms and spread it out for the digital generation to see. Some might think this is good and that children benefit when presented with anything and everything, every idea and opinion. It's not a good thing. But it is a reality and it will be even more real by the time they've left us to lead their world. What we do now while they are with us is important.

We must teach children to have a profound respect for our national heritage. The ideas and the principles created during those early days of our nation are timeless and are not subject to the aging process. Culture, opinion, political leaders, and popular ideas may change and shift.

But those who founded this nation and the documents created by the principles that shaped our freedom should be respected. No matter the mistakes we've made throughout our history, we must teach our children to exercise a profound respect for those documents and the thoughtful reasoning that produced them.

It seems that we now consider anyone who lived in the past to be irrelevant and even harmful. And by making them irrelevant, we may find ourselves declaring that any good done by them is to be discarded or rethought. But, just as none of us would survive a measurement of our lives by an accounting taken for one moment, one act or one idea, so we too must see that, even with their mistakes, the leaders who set a course for freedom in our nation should be honored and respected for crafting those documents to protect that freedom.

We always learned this in school. That doesn't mean it will continue. And it certainly doesn't mean that it will remain after we are gone.

One of the wisest things we can do in transferring wisdom to digital generations is to make sure we instill within the children and adolescents of these generations a profound regard for human life and a profound respect for our national heritage.

THE CURRICULUM

Some may take this environment of change and throw out things that should not be abandoned or modified. While *how* we teach must change, *what* we teach should not. We must reinforce, begin, or continue teaching classical curriculum to generations. We make no reference here to the methodology. We only address the curriculum, what we teach. Whether we educate in urban environments, STEM academies, technology-driven schools, classical schools, homeschools, or so many more, we should be teaching classical curriculum.

A simplistic view of education would draw a sharp distinction between two approaches to the teaching curriculum. One would be what is commonly referred to as progressive education. The thought is that it's a modern world and we should change curriculum accordingly.

The thought is to keep it current and relevant to the prevailing cultural feelings and acceptable opinions. The only important thing is the new thing. The only important knowledge is the functional knowledge to get along. Progressive reacts to the change.

The other would be an established and proven classical curriculum, which has existed for centuries. Classical, rather than being reactionary to the culture, is responsive to the culture but within a very defined understanding. We have to understand the crucial elements of this classical curriculum.

First, classical curriculum is a body of knowledge. It's content. It's what we teach, the scope and the sequence of what we teach and why we teach it. Most often, classical curriculum is perceived as a methodology. While some elements of practice may work best in a classical approach, methodology is not the heart of classical curriculum. Rather, classical curriculum is content, the curriculum.

Many speak of the trivium in classical curriculum. Actually, it's anchored in a double trivium (a three-pronged system). The first is the characteristics, the primary elements. This trivium is truth, goodness, and beauty. These characteristics can be blended into an overarching element called virtue.

Are we teaching students to be virtuous? Can we remain anchored in truth, objective truth, that is not subject to popular opinion or cultural demands? Are we leading students to an appreciation of beauty, an awareness of the best in all things? Do we teach students to practice goodness in every action and interaction?

This is virtue and virtuous. This is a classical trivium of character that forms the foundation for all learning.

We exist independently but we live in a community world. That community requires us to interact with others. And we should be able to do that effectively, morally, and for the good of others. As we teach, we transfer wisdom when we teach how to operate morally in the community.

But we short circuit a lot of growth if we move to the community too quickly. We must instill that moral sense intrinsically within the child first. Teaching the trivium of truth, goodness, and beauty is first an individual knowledge. A classical curriculum knows that we connect with the individual first. Then, as the individual establishes that moral center, the individual learns to respond effectively within the community.

We cannot flip that order. We don't teach the community good before the moral center of the individual. Doing so can lead to the individual being swayed by the current popular feelings of the community. A classical curriculum reaches the person first and moves the person to a community of people.

The curricular trivium is a sequential process. This trivium is chronological in order and it follows a prescribed path for the learner: grammar, logic, and rhetoric. We teach students language, proper and appropriate language, that communicates effectively and has layers of thought and learning embedded within.

This trivium is taught intentionally, following a pattern meant to address the three stages of learning. The grammar stage for the younger learner is composed of memorization, learning facts and acquiring knowledge during those earliest years of education. This establishes a base of knowledge.

The next stage, reserved primarily for the middle and intermediate years, is the logic stage. During these years, the learner is seeing themes and patterns in what they are learning. And, as this motivates the learner to start putting these together, a higher level of thinking occurs.

The third stage, rhetoric, is designed to elevate the learner to be engaged in dialogue, examination, learning through conversation and investigation. This is when the student becomes an independent learner with the capacity to personally learn.

Classical purists follow the trivium, sometimes in a parallel fashion, with the quadrivium. This is curricular as well. The quadrivium consists of arithmetic, music, geometry, and astronomy. When connected, these form the seven subjects for liberal arts.

Centuries ago, classical curriculum was committed to these seven subjects to create a full understanding of human studies, and many students moved to the study of theology, or even philosophy, once the liberal arts were completed. There was the idea, in early America, that this liberal arts focus would teach to the whole child, whether religious or philosophical pursuits would follow or not.

Now, a classical curriculum did not always confine itself to liberal arts in the early part of our country's history. Becoming a craftsman and skilled in specific areas was also important. Some subjects outside the liberal arts provided a practical and functional foundation for learners. Often, apprenticeships passed on some of this but there were also formal studies as well. However, the liberal arts scope and sequence followed a path for passing on the content to the student. For our purposes, let's look at three subjects on that path.

LITERACY

Knowing how to read is the most fundamental skill in learning. Reading intersects everything. It's often said that we learn to read so we can read to learn. The reader will stay engaged with learning his or her entire life.

While the modern effective reading level of common print in society may rise only to a sixth-grade level, we should never stop trying to improve skills in literacy with students. Learning to read is analogous to the discovery of fire in ancient civilizations. A new world is opened when we read. Why would we believe it's acceptable to only get learners to the minimum level just to survive?

The distinction between one who reads just enough to get by and one who reads more than enough to live by is exponential. The entire neurological framework is activated in a learner if we focus on literacy development. A classical curriculum knows first that the reading learner is a healthy learner.

What students read matters. A classical curriculum understands that the timeless is relevant to the present. Classical canons of literature have been produced through the centuries and modern, progressive attempts may be found wanting when placed on the same shelf as these classics.

Significant works can be found among the great pieces of literature if they have no agenda other than the advancement of the trivium elements of truth, goodness, and beauty. Do they teach all men and women a moral foundation?

Relevancy is nice. It's certainly important to know where we are in our cultural environment and stand ready to respond to the shifts and changes in that environment. Attempting to be relevant, though, loses significance if we believe that we must abandon the proven classical works of literature. The principles of goodness and virtue are taught through the classical stories, tales, and books.

While the complex layers of instruction are deep, the simple approach is that we teach language and reading in an explicit manner. We should teach knowledge about the English language and the background and the roots of the words. Much of our language derives from Latin backgrounds. Words are important and we should study the patterns and the reasons for the words.

Rote memorization and sight reading may satisfy the educator who looks only for the sounding out of words. However, we lose much when we do not dig into the roots of the language. And not digging in causes us to have a progressive "get it and move on" approach to literacy. This robs the learner of the reasons and patterns for the language. This is why Latin is important in classical curriculum. Everything had a purpose. That fits in the framework for all classical curriculum.

Teaching early the logic in language provides a foundation for the later instruction in logic for the learner. A classical curriculum is connected to the study of liberal arts in a world of logic and order. Literacy and reading, though certainly the linchpins of beauty and creativity, have embedded principles of that logic and order if taught in a sequential classical curriculum.

HISTORY

Social studies sit prominently in the classical classroom. Particularly in the study of civilizations that have existed throughout history, classical curriculum champions the tenet that what we learn from these civilizations teaches much about the world. Though societies rise and fall and the progress of technology advances throughout that same history, the principles we learn from these societies can inform us as we continue to work together.

A classical curriculum, rather than dismissing these civilizations as failures, digs deep into these studies to glean the significant and pull out the important. Students in classical studies have been able to find their place in the bigger picture. To ignore the studies of the world, and the historical societies that have existed in this world, is detrimental to the learner.

These are not mere cursory glances into these civilizations. These are studies that search for the trivium-specific elements. Whether through the literary artifacts or the documented records from these civilizations, the trivium of truth, goodness, and beauty is reinforced and proven when we study them.

We must study the Middle Ages, the Roman world, ancient civilizations. And through these studies, we can find the tremendous foundations laid for the period in our own history when a new nation was being formed. The authors of our founding documents understood classical content and fit their destiny within that framework.

MATHEMATICS

The classical approach to classical instruction is to orbit around an axis of logic and patterns. In other words, there is order. We are not random. But this order exists in a changing world. While experiencing these changes, a classical curriculum keeps the order and logic in the significant center for the child. Nowhere does this happen more strongly than in the study of math. While the order and patterns can be seen in all subjects, math sits at the epicenter of this instruction.

The study of math is the study of logic. No subject provides a formula for logic as effectively as the study of mathematics. Learners gain an advantage in problem solving when we first see math as the genesis for establishing these skills.

A classical curriculum understands the sequential order of problem solving. But even more, it understands that the learner can be taught to see everything as an equation rather than a problem. There is logic in sequenced mathematics. The adolescent learner, having been given a solid approach to logic, can independently utilize strategies as math becomes more complex.

Rather than the progressive state of current math instruction, which is relegated to a set of survival skills, a classical embodiment of math instruction fits the study of math within the entire framework of liberal arts academia. Everything connects together in this framework and math plays its part.

Teaching logic, patterns, and order is an important element of the overarching principle in classical curriculum. Just as the study of civilizations shows the patterns of man throughout historical records, the study of math embeds a sense of logic in the learner. While one may not ever actually "need" algebra, as so many math teachers told us long ago, one understands the world more clearly when the concepts, principles, and patterns of this mathematical logic are planted in the mind.

To understand that the world exists in a logical, patterned manner lends itself to the logical sense within the child to see how one may approach the varied and multiple issues that will be faced as an adult. If the learner is only taught to survive testing and the deeper strata of mathematical reasoning are not mined, the learner is denied the classical point of mathematics. Teaching math through a classical curriculum is crucial to the learner.

The math instruction is sequenced at early stages. While the earliest trivium concern is the establishment of grammar, math is not set aside as an extraneous subject. Rather, it's a complimentary companion to the element of grammatical instruction. Even as the patterns of man are learned through history, the patterns of music are learned through fine arts and the patterns of language are learned through literacy, so too are patterns learned through math.

METHODOLOGY

We have multiple pedagogy models in our country. While these methods of teaching may be vastly different, from structural ordering of teacher-to-student interactions to open classroom concepts that place student empowerment prominently out in front, we can still aim for those elements that will instill wisdom in our learners.

No matter the pedagogy, we must implement a classical curriculum that ensures our time spent with our students teaches the right and good things. We must place the virtuous elements of truth, goodness, and beauty as our priority in our curricular choices and our practice. This can be done on campuses committed to liberal arts and campuses aiming for studies in science, math, and engineering.

Shepherd heart teachers teach the right and good. Finding, training, and implementing a classical curriculum gives those teachers the tools and the content to plan and mentor their learners every day.

NOTES

1. "When Human Life Begins," April 17, 2017, https://www.acpeds.org/the-college-speaks/position-statements/life-issues/when-human-life-begins.

7

THE ACADEMIC PARALLEL STRUCTURE FOR THE SHEPHERD HEART TEACHER

As shepherd heart teachers for digital learners, there are some things we should do to structure the learning environments. Administrators and teachers have to think like architects in designing campuses and classrooms. The parallels of moral education and transformed learning systems for digital generations are just that: parallels. We will look later at how these parallels are woven together, but for now we will only address the academic parallel.

PRECISION MASTERY LEARNING SYSTEMS

As we've seen, technology has the opportunity to do so much for the classroom. However, it doesn't replace the teacher, only repositions that educator to provide a more engaged environment between learners and teachers. Leveraging the gifts and talents of intelligent teachers with the incredible capacity of emerging technology gives us the optimum opportunities for learning in the digital world. How does it look and how can we structure this?

We need to design what we call *Precision Mastery Learning Systems*. Mastery learning is key to all we do. We have already seen that measuring learning over teaching is the only true measurement for education. We can teach but do they learn? Mastery learning eliminates so many barriers that we had in the former teaching systems.

Leveraging technology doesn't mean that we *only* use technology. Instead, we design the classroom to ensure learning by using a blend of every resource. Some pieces of the learning environment will be technology rich and some will be teacher specific. The keys to both will be:

1. When do we use technology?
2. What does the technology do?
3. When do we use teachers?
4. What does the teacher do?

If the technology can do eight of the tasks formerly done by the busy teacher, leaving the teacher to engage with every student in a much more effective way, it doesn't control the learning nor the classroom. This is not Computer Ed 101. This is not computer learning. The technology doesn't perform miracles. The technology serves a purpose. It's a great tool for digital learners. And in that respect, it's *engaging on a cognitive level*. We have to use, rather than be used by, technology.

On the other side of that coin, what about the teacher? The teacher is a facilitator but the right kind of facilitator. Facilitation is the higher form of intentional engagement in the digital learning system. The teacher is the most gifted and the most committed person in the room. The teacher can perform miracles if we mix the ingredients correctly and give them the opportunity. And the teacher is *engaging on an emotional level*. We have to position them to make those connections even more effectively.

Mastery learning is our measurement. And the balance of technology and teachers is a formula we can design. If we want to get the most out of each, we have to achieve mastery learning systems without feeling the need to choose one over the either. They are both important.

Precision defines our design and moves the structure of the learning environment to a new level. But the word has an even deeper meaning. It identifies what we do as being precise while also being adaptable and flexible, not confining ourselves to one pedagogical option. Instead, we use all of these. We approach the design in a very precise way.

And we apply that precision in the classroom by not feeling we have to choose one option, pledge our loyalty and devotion to only that option, and stick with that option, accepting the fact that it won't work for some. In the precision approach, we believe in every option and we take the time and give it the attention to design the learning environment using every option.

How do we do that? By addressing the four key elements. In the Precision Mastery Learning System, we address when and what technology does as well as when and what the teacher does in the classroom. We do that by understanding that, for the digital learner, we can best achieve precision mastery by being precise about the when and what for each. And that requires that we pull out the instructional capacity for each.

THE DELIVERY SYSTEM FOR CONTENT IN PRECISION MASTERY LEARNING SYSTEMS

For our purposes, we draw a perception distinction between the concepts of *instruction* and *teaching*. The former systems were heavy on teaching mostly in the form of direct instruction that relied much on lecturing and controlling the delivery of content to learners. It's burdensome and awkward. It placed the teacher in the center and valued that placement above all else.

In transformed learning systems, we turn to the term *instruction* to define what we are doing in the classroom. To instruct, to transfer learning, is to take responsibility for learning. Instruction commits to the learning measurement.

Teaching looks at our job to see whether we prepared, presented, and performed the tasks. Instruction looks to the learner to see whether they've actually learned. So in the digital classroom, we look for instruction. And instruction takes many forms. A Precision Mastery Learning System is not self-paced. It's self-directed.

In Precision Mastery Learning Systems, we assign instructional components to both the teacher and the technology. We design it to meet the needs of digital generations. And we are particular and purposeful in the design. We identify four types of instructional delivery and we define each one specifically. Let's look at each one.

THE FOUR TYPES OF INSTRUCTION

Connectional Instruction

With connectional instruction, which is technology rich, the technology is used to deliver content and the learner reviews through reading and reviewing that content. It's curriculum, the modern version of the old textbook. Remember that technology engages learners and motivates students in many ways. Dry text and words on the screen have the ability to come alive if the creator of the content is skillful and produces an engaging digital environment for the learner.

We connect the student with the content through this delivery method. There's nothing wrong with technology taking over that delivery, if it's engaging. Now, we have to draw the distinction between engaging and entertaining. There is much to be said for gaming being used for learning. And if done right, it can be engaging and entertaining. The creators of those digital environments must take care to provide for rigorous learning.

For our purposes, though, we are addressing the fundamental, rigorous application of classical curriculum delivered through technology. Is the content addressing higher-level capacity for learners? Does it have adequate opportunities to check for understanding through quizzes and reviews? Is it sequenced effectively and does it cover the scope of the subject area for the grade level?

And is that curriculum created with a robust management system that doesn't buffer constantly? Can learners and teachers navigate the curriculum easily? Is it going to be efficient for learners to use as we empower them to learn what they should learn?

If all these things are so, why would we not want that technology to deliver the content? While we might appreciate the old hardcovers of our youth, what's so magical about a book? We do not need to fear the fact that technology probably delivers that content even better than we do.

Connectional instruction, in which the learner is reviewing and reading, is leveraging a technology strength. But it's also reinforcing something that is crucial for digital generations. While we may not be hurting students by not leveraging technology in a robust way in the classroom, it's important that we consider what we know about these generations.

Remember that we should be thinking about their well-being even after we are gone. In that world, technology is the forced way to get through the day. Accessing our finances, buying our groceries, so many things will depend on being able to use technology. If we see that coming in their future, we need to make wise choices for them now.

And this is more than just the occasional project. This is not just throwing in some computer time. Connectional instruction is using the technology as the primary delivery system for the classical curriculum. Every day and for every subject. It's the foundation for the learner.

- The students should be engaged with the delivery system.
- The students should be progressing effectively.
- The students should be meeting minimum requirements for mastery exams.

Elevational Delivery

Elevational instruction is technology rich and is the higher form of usage in which technology is used by learners to access sources and resources to research and learn new knowledge independently. There are multiple uses for technology in the classroom. The two primary sets of uses, though, are to deliver the curriculum (connectional) and to provide research opportunities for learners (elevational).

We elevate learners to a higher form of learning by training them to be researchers. While connectional instruction trains learners to be fluent in technology because it demands daily utilization of technology, elevational instruction trains the learner to be fluent in technology because it demands deeper, independent research using technology.

A simple example of this usage would be if a student needed to know how to measure the rate of slope. It's easy to ask the teacher. It's easy for the teacher to explain it and teach it to the student. But we short circuit the higher opportunity if we do not train them to access technology to find their answers. By accessing resources on the internet, the student has resources in which college professors, tutors, and other professionals have digital videos that can teach the student how to measure the rate of slope. And these can be used as often as needed by the learner.

This is not an insult to the teacher in the room, as long as the teacher knows that he or she is creating multilayered opportunities for the digital generations by adopting this approach. In fact, even if a teacher is addicted to preparing and presenting his or her lesson plans for learning, the opportunity is still there.

Teachers of digital can create their own videos. There are several resources for this online. The teacher can actually produce these easily and professionally. If a teacher does this for every lesson he or she would want to teach, why not take the time to produce these and have them uploaded and available for every student to access?

Doing that fills several needs. First, the teacher may still want to present his or her teaching to students. Second, the teaching is available and accessible for students twenty-four hours a day and on weekends, as well as during class time. Third, the students receive the instruction they need.

Lastly, and most important, the same instruction is available for the learner but the process of accessing it through technology doubles the best things we want to teach through elevational instruction. But we've done it without pacing, delaying, or hurting the progress of the entire class.

Learners should be trained to research for their answers a minimum of three legitimate times before finally seeking direct help from a classroom teacher. While it's important that we not pace learners, we should also not let them get bogged down. However, if they've legitimately tried at least three sources and they still haven't successfully gotten the help they need, the teacher can be allowed to directly teach the concept to the student. But we have to be firm about elevational instruction.

- The student has a list of resources to access for deeper learning and research.
- The student shows evidence of researching the sites.
- The student always goes to these resources first.

Directional Instruction

Directional instruction is teacher specific, in which the teacher provides some level of direct instruction, whether it be through lecture, dialogue, workshops, or others. Many in the education reform world may believe, and even state loudly, that any form of direct instruction is forbidden. That's just not the case.

There is value in some form of presentation from the teacher to learners. Remember that the key is to not hinder the progress of learners. And forcing learners to stay together is an organizational function for educators because allowing everyone to progress independently seems hard to manage. It's not difficult if you leverage the technology and the teacher accurately.

Directional instruction is successful as long as the teacher knows the class and knows the learner needs. For instance, as students progress independently through curriculum, the teacher may see the need to create a pullout or workshop during the week in which all students needing assistance, such as knowing how to measure the rate of slope or another specific concept, can stop and focus on the presentation.

The teacher provides directional instruction when he or she tutors or provides individual instruction to a learner. Going back to what we learned about elevational instruction, if the learner has made a minimum of three attempts to learn something by accessing resources online and still hasn't grasped the information or concept, the teacher can use directional instruction to the learner.

Additionally, as previously suggested, teachers can create their own archive of presentations and lectures, keeping these to a maximum of seven minutes. This is directional instruction.

The key element about directional instruction is that it must be kept to a minimum because it can prevent, delay, or hinder progress. It's not the teacher's teaching skills or abilities that are the problem. It's the fact that it forces learners to stay together. It robs the student of empowerment.

We need engaged educators with empowered learners. We need directional instruction sometimes, but even then, can we do this in creative ways in our classrooms? Teachers are intelligent people. They'll know how to do that in a way to not only engage with learners in a more effective way but to also embed the purposes of the learning system in their direct opportunities.

- The teacher intentionally plans a limited level of specific and particular things wherein there is some direct instruction involved.
- The teacher uses the time to create the instruction to support the personalized and independent learning process.

Positional Instruction

Positional instruction is the teacher positioning him- or herself as the creator and developer of specific projects and innovative learning opportunities. The system is not project based, but its projects are used as supplemental learning opportunities. The teacher plans and creates projects for deeper learning.

This is the teacher being the leader. Learners are on a journey and this type of instruction can increase their learning. Sometimes an external project can open eyes and minds to greater levels of learning. Positional instruction is an added benefit of the learning system that frees the teacher from the busy tasks formerly required in teaching systems.

We will discuss this later, but oral defenses are also wonderful opportunities for positional instruction. The teacher, positioned as a subject matter expert, has the opportunity to examine the knowledge capacity of a student and make a determination about moving to next mastery exams.

Whether the goal is projects connected to the subject matter, oral defenses to give students the right to take exams, or supplemental research assigned by the teacher, positional instruction is a significant part of the classroom in Precision Mastery Learning Systems.

- Oral defenses can be opportunities to assign and consider projects that will deepen learning and increase the understanding of students.
- Projects should not minimize or prevent progress for students, but rather should reinforce the progress and personalized elements.

THE CURRICULAR PROCESS OF PRECISION MASTERY LEARNING SYSTEMS

How does the learner get from the opening screen at the beginning of the curriculum to the final exam? What's the process of learning new content? It's important to know that, in Precision Mastery Learning Systems, while the empowering of students may seem to be losing some of the organized process of former teaching systems, the management of the curriculum process tightens up the organization.

First, the curriculum has to be organized, using the best pieces of technology potential. The curriculum can be the organized component

THE ACADEMIC PARALLEL STRUCTURE

that is scoped and sequenced to ensure that everything they need to know, they will learn. This is not difficult if the right curriculum developers are involved. It's written, created, and formatted for a digital world much the same way that hardcover textbooks are for the nondigital framework.

Every subject is covered. Every key element for the subject is included. It has a scope of information and a sequence to successfully learn these essentials. For our example, we can look at some models of this currently being used.

We can look at the typical biology requirement for secondary students. The content is sectioned into ten equal chapters. Every essential element for learning biology is sectioned into one of these ten chapters sequentially in order to provide a successful process to learn biology as well as to be prepared for high-stakes testing.

As the student begins, the curriculum is accessed online through digital means. The student has a laptop, a device, or desktop computer. The teacher assigns the particular chapter to each student.

The chapter is 10 percent of the content. The unit is designed to be engaging for learners and provides the sequenced progression from the first digital page to the last. Throughout the chapter, the student will have quizzes and reviews that deepen their learning and check for understanding. As the student takes these quizzes, they must pass and are allowed to use their ability to return and review the content during the quiz.

Students are allowed to work at their own ability level. And students are given the freedom to make their own decisions about what to work on. Learners may be sitting next to each other but be working on different subjects. Or they may be in the same subject but be at different places in the chapter.

And students are allowed to work together, alone, or with partners. The quizzes are graded, but these grades are not recorded in a grade book. These grades allow the student to continue moving forward through the chapter.

Why would we allow students to work together and why would we allow the students to use the chapter while taking these quizzes? Furthermore, why would not record their grades on quizzes?

Simply because there lies in the future the most important piece of the chapter in Precision Mastery Learning Systems: the mastery exam. That exam is the single most important thing. It's 10 percent of the final grade. It allows them to move to the next chapter.

A student eventually works through the entire chapter. The student is almost ready for the mastery exam. Almost.

Once a student has completed everything, he or she speaks with the teacher about scheduling an oral defense. This is where positional instruction comes in. The teacher schedules the time for the student to prove his or her learning. Why? Because in Precision Mastery Learning Systems, students must earn the right to take a mastery exam.

The teacher is allowed to develop his or her own oral defense instrument or process. This must be something that the teacher uses to determine if the learner is ready for the mastery exam. The oral defense can be a review that the teacher has created, a project that the student creates (such as a brief but significant paper), or some other method wherein the student proves that he or she has studied the content for the chapter and should be allowed to test.

For the mastery exam, everything is flipped. The mastery exam is in a testing room in which no one but the testing coordinator is allowed to enter. It's just the learner, the testing coordinator, and the test. No talking and no use of any resources or study materials. No phone, no device, and no help.

If the student has completed all the work and has proven, through the oral defense, that he or she is ready for the mastery exam, he or she may schedule the test. The student takes the test alone.

The only passing grade for progress is 90 percent. If the student scores less than 90 percent, he or she will have to return to the chapter, study, and schedule a second exam.

And the most important feature of the process is that this is the only grade entered in the grade book. Each result of the mastery exam attempts is recorded.

For instance, if a student scores 82 percent, the 82 is recorded for the student. However, the student is not allowed to move to the next chapter. He or she will have to schedule another exam. But the 82 remains on the books. The student, on the second attempt, must still score 90 percent in order to be allowed to progress. But the highest score the student can have recorded on the second attempt (and subsequent attempts) is 90.

So for this example, the student scores 82 and it's recorded. And on the second attempt, the student scores 100. The student receives a 90 in the grade book for the second exam. These two grades are averaged and the student's *final score for that chapter* is 86.

So continuing with the example, the first student received an official score of 90 for the unit and the second student received an official score of 86 for the chapter.

The reason for this process is that a student may score 90 the first time, thus receiving 90 for the chapter and is allowed to move to the next chapter. However, if a student scores 82 the first time, then scores 100 the second time, you must average those two and place the official score as that average. And allowing 90 as the highest grade after the first attempt keeps it fair.

The first student may have worked much harder for the first attempt and only required that one attempt to receive his or her score. So to be fair, the highest recorded score for attempts after the first time is 90. And while many would debate fairness, parents and students demand fairness when it concerns GPA and class rankings for particular honors and college requirements.

Meanwhile, the teacher is monitoring the learners and their progress through the digital learning management system. While student empowerment is crucial, no student is allowed to ignore subjects or content. Should the teacher notice this in the system, time is scheduled to engage with the student to discover why this may be occurring.

Students may finish subjects before the conventional end of the school year. Not a problem. We do not want to hinder progress. They are empowered to move to the next subjects and content.

That's the fundamental curricular process for Precision Mastery Learning Systems. While there is much more to the classroom, this process serves as the anchor for the system. Learning happens because we master the subject. And we leverage the technology and the teacher in a way that allows empowerment for students and engagement by teachers.

ARCHITECTURAL AGILITY EQUATIONS: EMPOWERING, ENGAGING, ENCOURAGING

Having the four types of instruction now in place in the classroom and having the curricular process in place and working, we now move to the architectural pieces. We have three structural components to position ourselves to best engage in the most optimum way. We call these the *three architectural agility equations*.

THE THREE ARCHITECTURAL AGILITY EQUATIONS

Agility Equation 1: Balancing Technology and Teachers

Each day, children are in a classroom and information must be delivered. Technology and teachers can be leveraged to provide the best learning environment. The learning experience is characterized by a blend of these primary delivery models. Teachers can provide so many distinctive, engaging, and creative teaching strategies. Conversely, technology can do the same. But we have to find that balance.

So often, we consider strategies and plans across the board. We purchase equipment and initiate the usage the same for every classroom and every teacher. It's a district matter but it affects each individual classroom. Knowing that, when the classroom door closes, the teacher will end up doing what is best for the student, we have to leverage everything, but we have to personally resolve how much technology and how much teacher we need for every classroom. That's the task of the campus administrator.

And just as everyone has strengths and weaknesses, gifts and abilities, expertise and experience, personalizing everything (including the teacher) to leverage those elements based on the uniqueness of the educator in the classroom can have the most benefit.

Now, the teacher doesn't make these decisions. The school leaders should. Just as we expect teachers to personally know every student, we should expect the school leader to know every teacher. Being able to see the system as a personalized learning environment, the school leader should be able to create the best blend for each classroom individually.

While some might believe it's best to roll out technology systemically and force the same plan, the same way, for every teacher, it doesn't work if we are truly wanting the environment in which the shepherd heart teacher can best utilize the resources. As administrators, we personalize our environments for educators the same way we expect teachers to personalize learning experiences for each learner.

That's classroom architecture. The first equation falls to the school leader, whether it be a superintendent, principal, or school director. Transforming from teaching systems to learning systems can be done and there's a way to plan it, train it, and implement it successfully. It falls to the school leader to address classroom architecture.

Agility Equation 2: The Altitude of the Teacher

What will be the required engagement the teacher must take for each individual learner and what will be the required empowerment the teacher must give each individual learner in the classroom? We use "flight plan" to define this and "altitude" of the teacher to describe this because it can be better understood if we compare to that analogy.

The Satellite

Some students will need little engagement because they thrive in environments in which they are given freedom and empowerment. We monitor the progress of the learner, interject when necessary to give guidance, and make sure they are progressing. These students need maximum empowerment and little engagement academically. We are like a GPS system, a satellite that watches and gives guidance when important things need to be offered to the learner, but we don't get in the way and hinder their progress.

The Airliner

Other students will need more academic engagement. They depend on us to take a much more involved and engaged approach. We may have to assist in setting the plan, help in the progress, and even assist in some of the decision making. These are students that will progress and learn but we will have to limit the empowerment at times and increase the engagement academically in order to see effective progress. We are much like airline pilots for these learners. They need us to help them navigate their journey. To get where they are going, they will depend on us to be engaged at some level.

The Crop Duster

And then we will have those students who must have maximum academic engagement every day. While still needing some level of empowerment, we have to remain engaged or they will not do well. We will need to be hands on and we need to be that way on a daily basis. We describe this as a crop duster that flies low over the field and drops the necessary ingredients on the field in order for it to flourish and/or survive. We have to stay engaged consistently with these learners.

The second structural equation is for the teacher. Learners are different and each will need some level of engagement and some level of empowerment in order to learn effectively.

Agility Equation 3: Freedom and Fences

Empowerment is freedom. But some learners don't respond to academic freedom as well as others. Maybe it's self-discipline or an insufficient foundation of previous material or maybe it's behavioral issues. But some learners may need some fences.

The third agility equation addresses the individual learner. "Freedom and fences." A learner has access to content. We have been created to learn and content can be delivered. And the learning capacity is personalized in the learner.

Rather than molding to a teaching style, learners in a learning environment benefit from a personalized opportunity. If we know that learning is personalized, we have to also know that learners are not going to respond the same.

We must champion student empowerment. We are breaking away from the "same pace" mentality. Though it makes the organization of the learning system a bit more complex, we have to empower students in decision making and content progress.

But as it is said, *Pacing is poison but drowning is just as dangerous*. In other words, we can't leave them alone to drown in discouragement and failure to progress. Empowerment doesn't mean leaving them alone. We must be engaged. And that engagement is focused on the learner.

We cannot abandon our responsibility for the sake of looking like we are innovative. Don't forget, the measurement of innovation is not the number of computers, it's not the cool technology, and it's not the lack of lecture. Even though shepherds moved sheep to new pastures without fences, eventually some fencing had to be built.

At this juncture of change and transformation, we have to know that the opportunity to give more focused time for the teacher is the opportunity to give more engagement time for the learner. Yes, we should empower the learner. And it's best to consider that freedom first and foremost.

But building fences isn't the greatest mistake if the learner needs some fences.

How much structure will this student need to progress? It would be nice to generalize our environment and have students conform to "room rules," meant to apply to everybody equally. But that's not the reality of the transformed learning system. We have to always resolve the third agility equation. How much freedom, and how much fencing, does this student need?

THE GLOSSARY OF PRECISION MASTERY LEARNING SYSTEMS

Shepherd Heart Teacher

An instructor who understands that mentoring, monitoring, managing, and measuring are qualities necessary for engagement. However, the teacher takes responsibility for the *learning* of the student, not the *teaching* of the subject. While the teacher is a subject matter expert, the passion and commitment is to the student.

The teacher is concerned with transferring wisdom to students while sharing information and providing knowledge are given their proper place in classrooms. The shepherd heart teacher adheres to an external moral code and the belief system of the teacher is not used as a proselytizing agent, but rather is used to inform and guide the practice and engagement of the teacher to the student.

Instruction and Teaching Paradigm

Teachers are still the most valuable element in classrooms. However, while the historical narrative of education demanded a teaching system that leaned heavily on preparation and presentation of lecture styles in classrooms because of limited resources, the current and emerging resources provide better opportunity to engage with learners in a personalized manner.

Transferring and transmitting information and content can be done leveraging technology and teachers. The concept of this transferring paradigm no longer means simply direct teaching, but rather embodies the concept of instruction.

Everything done in the learning system, everything done through moral education, and everything done through empowerment and engagement falls into the paradigm of instruction. This underlines everything the shepherd heart teacher does for digital learners.

Transformation over Education Reform

The paradigm that doesn't tweak or modify traditional teaching systems but rather creates new strategies and process for learning. Rather than simply modifying a teaching system, in which any innovation or technology supports or reinforces that teaching, Precision Mastery is predicated on a transformed understanding rather than an education reform strategy.

Knowledge Inquiry

The process used by a learner who reads, researches, or reviews to find answers to questions.

Knowledge Analysis

The process used by a learner who digs and dives into information to gain knowledge.

Oral Defense

The process in which learners must present their request to take a mastery exam, sufficiently prove their readiness, and receive approval from the educator to schedule and take the exam.

Mastery Exam

The graded high-stakes exam that proves learning of specific content, material, and curriculum. This is the only recorded grade and the minimum score for progress is 90 percent.

Chapter

An organized and trustworthy portion of subject matter, age appropriate and sequenced, that will add new knowledge to prior knowledge. Each chapter has reviews, quizzes, content, and mastery exams designed to move the learner to new levels of knowledge.

Precision Mastery Learning System

A learning system designed to leverage technology and teachers in the classroom. The system is delivered and measured through technology. The system values learning over teaching. The system is "precision" because of the design elements of the educator to engage with the learner, monitor progress, and determine the balances for the classroom as well as the student. The educator utilizes the four types of instruction.

Four Types of Instruction

- **Connectional**
  Technology is used to deliver content and the learner reviews through reading and reviewing that content.
- **Elevational**
  Technology is used to access sources and resources to research and learn new knowledge independently.
- **Directional**
  The teacher provides some level of direct instruction, whether it be through lecture, dialogue, workshops, or others.
- **Positional**
  The teacher plans and creates projects for deeper learning.

Moral Education

The commitment to a moral code that values objective truth and focuses on a moral classroom, not subject to relativism or subjective judgments that shift with current culture. Rather than a focus on self-esteem and self-focused practice, students are taught morality and the duty to first live rightly and justly before, and for, all men.

Moral education follows the patterns and understandings of the common good and behavior that values truth, goodness, and beauty that were common elements of good education for centuries but have seen a steady decline in recent history.

Academic Balance

When a learner is progressing through chapters at a healthy pace while addressing every subject in an effective manner, not ignoring any subjects.

Progress

The authentic measurement for learning. If the system has reliable measurements that ensure learning, the most optimum assessment for genuine learning is to measure progress. If the passing standard has high expectations, measuring long-term progress is more effective than subjective grading or measuring short-term performance.

Four Determinants

The four major elements to prove or measure innovation. These determinants are:

1. *Time*
   How is learning affected by time or time constraints? Bells, subject periods, schedules, calendar?
2. *Location*
   How is learning affected by location? Can content be delivered or learning occur in places other than the classroom or campus?
3. *Measurement*
   How is learning measured? Does the measurement actually measure learning and progress?
4. *Delivery*
   How is content delivered to the learner? Technology, teacher, textbooks?

Socratic Questioning

An engaged educator process in which the educator develops a higher level of questioning that goes beyond "business" level, one dimensional, yes and no responses. This process utilizes the concept of "language dancing"[1] to ignite the mind of the learner.

Socratic questioning is a systematic, rather than fragmented, process that creates reflective inquiry. It causes the learner to think beyond a single layer of concepts presented and connect thoughts leading to critical thinking. This is a learner taking the concept, turning it over in the mind, and monitoring, assessing, and evaluating what's being learned.

Socratic questioning is especially important for large group disciplines such as pullout sessions and direct teaching opportunities, and it is particularly useful for the oral defense.

The Five C Types of Questions for a Socratic Engagement

- Challenging the learner in a shepherding, thoughtful manner.
- Consequences of the concept to get the learner to think more deeply.
- Clarifying the thinking to make sure the learner is organized and analytical.

- Countering the point in a nonconfrontational manner to see every angle of the issue.
- Considering the question to get the learner to comprehend his or her answers and results.

Biopsy and Autopsy Testing

Autopsy testing is standardized testing and testing conditions at the *end of the learning process*. At this point, the test is a performance-based test to determine whether learning has occurred. Autopsy testing is not the optimal option because everything is standardized at the end, when nothing can be done to help the learner improve. The measurement only provides a snapshot of the performance.

Biopsy testing is standardized testing and test conditions at the *beginning of the learning process*. The process accurately measures the current state of the learner related to the subject matter. Everything can be standardized in biopsy testing because the measurement can be prescriptive and provide learners with immediate and ongoing treatments to improve learning. This can provide opportunities to diagnose strengths and deficiencies to structure optimum learning opportunities. This is an authentic measurement option.

NOTES

1. C. M. Christensen, M. B. Horn, and C. W. Johnson, *Disrupting Class: How Disruptive Innovation Will Change the Way the World Learns*, second ed. (New York: McGraw Hill, 2011).

8

THE EDUCATION THEORY FOR TRANSFORMED LEARNING SYSTEMS

SHEPHERD HEART INSTRUCTIONAL FRAMEWORK THEORY (SHIFT)

Education in the digital world will best be achieved and sustained by designing learning systems leveraging emerging digital resources and engaged educators, who serve as attainable and relevant moral exemplars taking responsibility for the academic and moral development of the learner while the instructional process is anchored in classical curriculum and delivered to the learner through technology.

There is a great need to transform education from standard and traditional teaching systems to relevant and effective learning systems that meet the requirements for mandated testing, instill the timely and proven elements of morality and wisdom, elevate the learner to a greater opportunity for participation in life beyond the classroom, and teach students to manage a digital world for the immediate and the future.

SHIFT is an architectural process wherein the disconnect from high-level intellectual research and practical implementation is eliminated and the best of each is explored, designed, and put into practice. This framework, rather than employing an unyielding set of itemized and systemic characterizations that cannot respond to each learner, utilizes a flexible and responsive system that teaches educators to be architects using a set of principles and guidelines that are nonnegotiable.

The architect is equipped with a set of tools, skills, and training to respond effectively to each learner. The learner is equipped with a classical curriculum, tools, and environment for effective progress. The campus is designed to create a sensed curriculum, not visible but affective culturally, of wisdom and morality that informs every plan, action, and outcome. The premise of the campus is that a classical curriculum, emerging digital resources, and educators committed to moral exemplar work will create a foundation of trusted and relevant education opportunity for new generations of learners.

THE QUALITIES OF SHIFT

The Closed Loop Aggregate System

SHIFT is first an education theory based on a *parallel architectural model* interweaving moral education with Precision Mastery Learning Systems. These two nonnegotiable parallels are not separate entities but are interdependent and fused together to create a closed loop system with an aggregate feedback and output relationship.

The output from each parallel loops back portions into the other to create the desired outcomes. Therefore, while some might see only the academic benefits of the learning system, it's not possible to simply separate this from the moral education component. Doing so may create improved academic outcomes, but the moral reasoning and moral intelligence of the learner remains subject to the threats of cultural conditioning.

Some might want to separate the moral education component from the learning systems. Doing so may increase moral thinking and elevate behavior morally but will leave the learner absent the capacity to navigate digital learning opportunities as an academic. The two parallels lose their separateness within the process and each loops portions of their benefits and outcomes back into the model.

The "Whole Teacher" Instructional Process

SHIFT is an *instructional framework* wherein every component of the aggregated system, working as one unit, relies on the concept of "instruction" as an intentional and worthy goal for every educator. Rather than focusing on the former role of teaching, defined as direct-heavy lectures and learner listening, every member on the campus is engaged with instructing, defined as a blended system of mentoring, monitoring, and guiding the learner in moral reasoning and motivated learning.

This is defined as *"whole teacher" engagement.* This framework of instruction is a comprehensive system that informs the teacher and the student in whole day focus on elevating the moral reasoning and the learner capacity to thrive in a digital world.

The Shepherd Heart Teacher

SHIFT identifies the educator as a shepherd heart teacher. This paradigm is an intentional practice by the educator to take responsibility for the moral development and academic success of the learner. The shepherd heart teacher is a particular identity that sets the educator apart from conventional expectations that are largely academic in nature.

The identity recognizes that education is transforming to learning systems and also perceives the need to develop moral character that addresses participation in a digital world. A shepherd heart teacher is defined as the following:

- An educator adhering to a moral code that informs and guides practice and engagement with learners.
- The moral code of the educator is not a proselytizing agent, but rather is the agent that perceptually connects the mental, spiritual, and emotional elements of the learner in the "teacher to learner" paradigm.

The Moral Centered Engagement

SHIFT is a *moral education theory* based on former concepts of educating students on a foundation of morality development. The theory, connected to studies in cultural movements in a digital world and responding to the need to educate students not only in academic but moral development as well, intentionally engages the teacher in the concept of moral responsibilities to the learner. This paradigm is defined through two primary elements of instructional responsibility.

- **The definition of a facilitator in transformed learning systems**

  The concept of "facilitator," rather than being known as a "guide on the side," is promoted and trained as *an elevated and accelerated engagement agent* in the classroom.

  While the former teaching systems, focused on the concepts of teaching as a task-heavy job that allowed teaching whether learning occurred or not, the transformed learning systems now create a balance of technology and teachers that offers the opportunity for elevated engagement between students and educators.

  Therefore, the facilitator can now leverage the resources to design the classroom more intelligently and intentionally create those engagement opportunities to keep the learner progressing academically and increasing his or her moral development. The facilitator is therefore the key element of a transformed learning environment.

- **The definition of relevant moral exemplars**

  The concept of being an attainable and relevant exemplar is the highest form of instructional engagement. The educator develops the "whole teacher" approach on the campus and in the classroom.

  This approach, rather than being a pseudo-disciplinary and behavioral system, connects to the passion and motivation of the educator to reach the learner through moral development and teach the learner through the intentional instructional framework.

  The digital world has an overarching intrusiveness in the shaping and forming of opinions and thoughts of the user. Digital generations are comfortable and affected users and must navigate this intrusiveness.

  While most efforts to produce relevant exemplars look outside the campus for examples to present to students for moral development, SHIFT looks to the teacher as the prime attainable and relevant moral exemplar.

The Educational Architectural Design

SHIFT is an *educational architecture theory* focused on appropriately defined concepts relevant to digital generations and emerging opportunities:

- The concept of learning over teaching. While the former systems promoted teaching as the primary role of the educator, SHIFT promotes learning as the ultimate measurement for all academic pursuits.
- The concept of instruction as a whole teacher process that replaces the lecture-heavy process of teaching.
- The concept of facilitation becomes a primary role of a learning systems educator.
- The educator takes on the responsibility of being an attainable and relevant moral exemplar on the campus and in the classroom.

The Attainable and Relevant Moral Exemplar

- The educator is the primary attainable and relevant exemplar and engages with the learner as such in every aspect. While exceptional exemplars have traditionally been known to produce motivation in moral development, recent studies show that these may be losing their effect in digital generations. [1]
- These same studies point to attainable and relevant exemplars as being more effective in producing motivation for character and moral development. [2] Rather than looking beyond the campus for these exemplars, the educator takes on the responsibility to be this relevant moral exemplar.
- The relevant moral exemplar engages in the classroom and on the campus with a focused attention on morality and wisdom. Two primary features of this attention to wisdom will be to produce within the learner a profound regard for human life and a profound respect for the historical national narrative.

The Precision Mastery Learning System

The learning system is mastery based and self-directed. Students are empowered to make decisions about their learning and are engaged with particular types of classroom instruction.

- *Connectional*
  Technology is utilized by learners to access curriculum.
- *Elevational*
  Technology is utilized by learners for deeper research.
- *Directional*
  Teachers utilize levels of direct and indirect instruction.
- *Positional*
  Teachers utilize projects and assigned measures to increase learning.

The system utilizes classical curriculum and digital delivery to vertically align successful learning opportunity with the development of digital research skills. Students are allowed to progress at their unique pace while being monitored by educators. Educators mentor and engage with students intentionally in order to provide a shepherding element with every student.

The system requires students to progress through sequenced curriculum and allows students to work cooperatively as they progress. The educator schedules and conducts an oral defense for any student requesting permission to take a mastery exam for each curriculum sequence. Learners, having gained permission, will take the mastery exam in isolation. The student must score 90 percent on the mastery exam to be allowed to move to progressive sequences.

The Foundational Values[3]

The development of moral reasoning will value the following outcomes in learners:

- *Knowledge*
  Seek and use the best knowledge, drive change that benefits others, and exemplify humility and intellectual honesty.
- *Passion*
  Find fulfillment in your life by improving the lives of others.
- *Responsibility*
  Take responsibility for your own life. No one will ever be as concerned about your success as you.
- *Be Principled*
  Always act with integrity, respect, and toleration.

- *Sound Judgment*
  Use economic thinking to create the greatest benefit while using the least resources.
- *Win-Win Focus*
  Cooperation creates real value in society—for yourself and others.
- *Opportunity*
  You make your own opportunities.
- *Freedom*
  Respect the rights of others and study the links between freedom, entrepreneurship, and societal well-being.

GLOSSARY OF SHIFT

Knowledge Inquiry
When a learner reads, researches, or scans to find answers to questions.

Knowledge Analysis
When a learner digs and dives into information to gain knowledge.

Oral Defense
When learners present their request to take a mastery exam, sufficiently prove their readiness, and receive approval from the educator to schedule and take the exam.

Mastery Exam
The graded high-stakes exam that proves learning of specific content, material, and curriculum. This is the only recorded grade and the minimum score for progress is 90 percent.

Transformation over Education Reform
The paradigm that doesn't tweak or modify traditional teaching systems, but rather creates new strategies and process for learning.

Chapter
An organized and trustworthy portion of subject matter, age appropriate and progressive, that will add new knowledge to prior knowledge. Each chapter has reviews, quizzes, content, and mastery exams designed to move the learner to new levels of knowledge.

Academic Balance

When a learner is progressing through chapters at a healthy pace while addressing every subject in an effective manner, not ignoring any subjects.

Progress

The authentic measurement for learning. If the system has reliable measurements that ensure learning, the most optimum assessment for genuine learning is to measure progress.

Four Determinants

The four major elements to prove or measure innovation. These determinants are:

1. *Time*

    How is learning affected by time or time constraints? Bells, subject periods, schedules, calendar?

2. *Location*

    How is learning affected by location? Can content be delivered or learning occur in places other than the classroom or campus?

3. *Measurement*

    How is learning measured? Does the measurement actually measure learning and progress?

4. *Delivery*

    How is content delivered to the learner? Technology, teacher, textbooks?

Precision Mastery Learning System

A learning system designed to leverage technology and teachers in the classroom. The system is delivered and measured through technology. The system values learning over teaching. The system is *"precision"* because of the design elements of the educator to engage with the learner, monitor progress, and determine the balances for the classroom as well as the student. The educator utilizes four types of instruction.

Moral Education

The commitment to a moral code that values objective truth and focuses on a moral classroom, not subject to relativism or subjective judgments that shift with current culture. Rather than a focus on self-esteem and self-focused practice, students are taught morality and the duty to first live rightly and justly before, and for, all men. Moral education follows the patterns and understandings of the common good and behavior that values truth, goodness, and beauty that were common elements of good education for centuries but have seen a steady decline in recent history.

Four Types of Instruction

- **Connectional**
  The technology is used to deliver content and the learners review through reading and reviewing that content.
- **Elevational**
  The technology is used by learner to access sources and resources to research and learn new knowledge independently.
- **Directional**
  The teacher provides some level of direct instruction, whether it be through lecture, dialogue, workshops, or others.
- **Positional**
  The teacher plans and creates projects for deeper learning.

Biopsy and Autopsy Testing

Autopsy testing is standardized testing and testing conditions at the end of the learning process. At this point, the test is a performance-based test to determine whether learning has occurred.

Biopsy testing is standardized testing and test conditions at the beginning of the learning process. The process accurately measures the current state of the learner related to the subject matter. This can provide opportunities to diagnose strengths and deficiencies to structure optimum learning opportunities. This is an authentic measurement option.

Shepherd Heart Teacher

An instructor who understands that mentoring, monitoring, managing and measuring are qualities necessary for engagement. However, the teacher takes responsibility for the learning of the student, not the teaching of the subject. While the teacher is a subject matter expert, the passion and commitment is to the student. The teacher is concerned with transferring wisdom to students while sharing information and providing knowledge are given their proper place in classrooms.

Architectural Equations

The three equations that must be solved for transformed schools.

The Classroom Balance of Technology and Teacher

Determining the level of technology and teacher engagement for each personalized classroom. This is typically performed by the administration.

The Altitude of the Teacher

Determining the level of engagement for each learner.

With some students, the teacher can act as a satellite that monitors the learner but provides direction and counsel when needed because the learner progresses effectively and independently.

With some students, the teacher can act as an airliner that provides more engagement but doesn't control beyond what is needed. The learner just needs some direct guidance and counsel occasionally. However, the teacher must be more engaged or the learner may not end up where he or she is meant to go.

With some students, the teacher must act as a crop duster. The teacher must fly low over the field and provide extensive engagement for the learner. The learner needs direct help frequently. The engagement is intentional.

Freedom versus Fences

The amount of freedom given to each student for optimum learning. Some students need more structure. They need fences or they will not progress effectively. Sometimes students can function better in an empowered environment. The teacher must determine how much freedom versus how much structure each student needs.

NOTES

1. C. James, *Young People, Ethics, and the New Digital Media: A Synthesis from the Good Play Project* (Cambridge, MA: MIT Press, 2009).

2. H. Han, J. Kim, C. Jeong, and G. Cohen, "Attainable and Relevant Moral Exemplars Are More Effective Than Extraordinary Exemplars in Promoting Voluntary Service Engagement," *Frontiers in Psychology* 8 (2017), doi:10.3389/fpsyg.2017.00283.

3. Youth Entrepeneurs, ed., "About YE: Our Foundational Values," 2017, https://youthentrepreneurs.org/about/about-us.

9

MODELS OF THE THEORY

The Shepherd Heart Instructional Framework Theory has, within it, many moving parts stretching across the spectrum from simple to complex. While theory is important, in the past we've experienced the disconnect that often occurs between research and practice. There seems to be a genuine intent on the part of researchers and practitioners where theory is articulated, and even accepted, but it falls apart at the point of implementation.

We've said before that "implementation trumps intent." None of the discontent is caused by a lack of intent from research or educators. It may just be the result of the immediacy necessary for meeting standards. It may be the result of high-level decision making that doesn't have the same priorities as in-classroom educators. The disconnect can also be caused by the fear of risk taking.

Whatever the reason may be, we often find that theory articulates the need and educators agree with the results, but actually creating the change or transformation in learning environments never happens. That's not because teachers don't want it. No teacher would deny learners what they feel would be greater opportunities. But that disconnect remains.

Most often, we find that, rather than a full implementation in a broad and effective way, change is done in pieces. This doesn't actually transform schools from teaching systems to learning systems. There's just enough change to call it change. But full transformation just doesn't occur.

The greatest hope for making theory real and effective is to provide real models. Often, when introducing theory, educators do what educators should do. They asked the question, "What does this look like?" Being able to see what the theory looks like, see how it behaves, and walk among the learners and educators engaged with the reality of the theory can reconnect the disconnect between research and practice.

Educators need to see it working. They need to ask questions and watch it in action. They are intelligent professionals and they know the questions to ask. They know what to look for and how to examine the theory firsthand.

All of us are in this together. Public, private, districts, charters, homeschools. These are our children and we must work together for these generations. Though charters have much the same requirements as traditional districts, there is an environment for taking risks that might not be available for those districts. If we can create the model for observation, we might be able to move all of us closer to the transformation needed for digital generations.

Urban, suburban, and rural children and adolescents are counting on us to do our best. We need examples, models in which the intelligent educator can see the implementation and know how to move from the intent to the reality. Yes, the implementation has to be configured to fit different populations with different needs, but the significant thing is to let the educator see it and start putting his or her intelligence to work to make this happen for his or her learners.

We must find answers for inner-city children. We must find answers for rural learners. And we must find answers for suburban students.

Our only response to those trying has to stop pointing out the obvious and visible distinctions between the populations they serve. We must stop pointing at the home conditions and social status as being the sole reason for the unavoidable cognitive destiny of the learner. Some live in nice neighborhoods and have their own car by the time they are old enough to drive. Some didn't have dinner the night before.

But if we generalize and pronounce success or failure based only on those conditions, we refuse to learn from each other and we refuse to sit at the same table with educators just trying to do good things for kids. This is not the time for adults to be defensive about their own castles and offensive in their efforts to knock anything else in order to somehow make themselves appear right, and solely right. We must play nice together in the sandbox.

Everyone has answers, but no one has *the* answer. We, as adults, have a shelf life and we won't be here long. These generations will live on after us. May we not leave a diminished legacy of being known only as a defensive generation of offensive adults who cared more about our own territory and backyard than we did about actually leaving behind a better opportunity for our children.

We have to come to the table together. We have to disarm ourselves, leaving our weapons of pride at the door and our agendas at home. We have to become learners again and learn together.

If we would stop taking ourselves too seriously and start taking the moral and cognitive health of digital generations seriously instead, we will leave them better off after we are gone. Will their grandchildren live in a better world because they attended our schools long ago?

It's possible. But it will require that we learn from each other. At the end of the day, there are no wins or losses. There's only the next generations we leave behind. Let's learn from each other.

We have great models scattered around the country but the model for the Shepherd Heart Instructional Framework Theory requires the following:

- an intentional focus on moral and wisdom education;
- an intentional focus on blended pedagogy connected to transformed learning and teaching; and
- a foundation of classical curriculum and content in all subjects.

Shepherd Heart Educational Design

Moral and Wisdom Education
Merged with Blended Learning Environments

- Educators are defined and engaged through a process aligned with personal belief systems specifically identified as an external moral code consisting of the elements of truth, beauty, goodness, and virtue.
- Teacher practice that instills the sensed curriculum of morality and wisdom that trains teachers to be relevant and attainable moral exemplars.

- Planned and intentional curricular events designed to study and explore extraordinary moral exemplars.
- Student development focused on moral reasoning informing behavior, emotion, and thought.

Shepherd Heart Instructional Framework Theory

Precision Mastery Learning Systems

- The curriculum is digitally delivered through technology and students access the content for every subject to progress sequentially through every subject.
- The students are empowered to make decisions on time spent in each subject daily.
- The students are empowered to make decisions to be engaged through various choices ranging from isolated learning to cooperative learning daily.
- The teachers monitor student progress consistently through technology platforms.
- The teachers engage with students regularly to ensure learning progress.
- The teachers create oral defense critiques for students seeking permission to take mastery exams.
- The students, upon completion of chapters and acceptable oral defense, are allowed to take mastery exams for each sequential chapter in every subject.
- The students are allowed to advance through their studies at their particular capacity.

Teacher Training and Focus

There should be three teacher preparation levels:

1. Each educator is expected to have sufficient requirements of higher education training from their personal career development.
2. Educators receive effective training in the learning system management for curriculum management and system navigation.
3. Each educator receives personal and focused training in moral education development.

FINAL THOUGHTS

Transforming education is hard work. It's hard enough just being a teacher. And sometimes it may seem like the never-ending voices are nothing but incessant reminders that we can always do better and always be different. It's the man who walks up on the scene and never rolls up his sleeves to help but certainly seems to know how to tell you what to do.

The hope is that you would know your value as an educator. Be encouraged that technology isn't going to replace you. The teacher is needed now more than ever. And you're too important to be marginalized or compromised.

Your ability to change lives is more possible now. Your skills lie in your ability to engage with every learner. You have that intrinsic challenge that undergirds everything you do and think, that passion that drives you forward and keeps you excited about being someone who has the influence and the opportunity to affect generations. That's a huge responsibility but it's also a great way to spend your life.

Be encouraged. If you as a shepherd heart teacher can know that what you do when you engage with students will change their lives, and the useful technology is your best friend, giving you the time to do that even more, you should be encouraged.

Shepherd heart teachers are out there. Let's give them what they need and let them do their jobs. Digital generations will need wisdom. Digital generations will need unyielding morality. Where will they get these? From those men and women who have the heart of a shepherd.

10

THE ANCHOR OF MORALITY AND WISDOM IN EDUCATING DIGITAL LEARNERS

An apologetic for moral education submitted for shepherd heart teachers with a humble confidence in the transference of virtue and goodness in a twenty-first-century digital classroom

Teaching the young is a sacred honor and sobering responsibility. While acknowledging that all are created to learn, and therefore each child and adolescent will naturally mature in his or her cognitive capacity and knowledge acquisition, those committed to guide, direct, and provide such must also acknowledge the gravity and the weight of that commitment.

As the modern world changes, timeless truths remain. These are bound within natural law and a moral understanding known by all men and have anchored all creation from ancient time to the present. Though typically defined as religious in nature, these truths are not merely confined by one's religious preference, but rather through the moral agreements of all men to prevent bad behavior and inspire personal good behavior. These are not subject to the personal or collective negotiations of men but stand as unassailable foundations for human interaction and instruments of peace and goodwill.

Those who teach must feel genuinely that these significant elements are points of navigation and lamps of illumination for all teaching. The body of content and information may increase, edit, or change as science and needs dictate, but the duty to teach the classical precepts and principles of morality remain. Therefore, those who teach must intentionally address, compose, and implement these daily, internally in actions of the individual and externally as members and participants of a community.

It is vital to the health of the nation, and to the agreed direction of all teaching provided by the educators of this nation, that there be communicated an established articulation of these for all who will devote themselves to our work. And rather than being a document of freedom for individual interpretation, this articulation is the collective *declaration of dependence* upon these principles to guide us in teaching young learners, now and in our future.

Assembling thought and conceptual framework for such a document requires trustworthy supportive material and content base. What proven reference documents and reflection would we use? Though the choice and adoption may vary between, and even among, groups of individuals, those who teach and lead would do well to depend primarily on a specific point of reference, one that has not lost its significance nor its relevance, even in the face of changing culture and diverse populations.

These address traditional and time-honored belief systems, communicating a reliance on classical truths and the modern practice applying those truths in educating children and adolescents. These points can be found in the principles and precepts guiding the founding fathers of this nation.

Those instrumental in the creation of a democratic and free country were best positioned to establish significant things before and while putting pen to paper. Having experienced the punitive burdens of governmental rule, the colonial populations of early America knew the harsh realities of shackled and fettered freedom. While escape from these shackles provided the motivating energy to seek a new land, once here, the colonials became increasingly aware that freedom was not afforded as a geographical surety.

The suffocating presence of government aggression and the increase of independent progression that lay within the hearts of those responsible for leadership in the original thirteen colonies engaged these men as architects for the creation of a society that suited the proliferation of the best that might be realized.

As the debates, considerations, and ideas began funneling toward a sharp distinction to, and separation from, the forced hand of government dictates, these brave individuals and communities expressed their understanding of this society, carefully analyzing the formation of this nation to offer not only opportunity but also a peaceful existence for citizens.

Guarding against the oppressive intervention of government rule, receiving fair and rightful treatment from even the smallest of government entities while encouraging honest and virtuous practice between members of the community, these men were significantly informed and guided by a set of principles. They did not apologize for acknowledging a dependence on certain and specific articles to direct their thoughts as they created original documents and expressions of true freedom.

As we consider our best opportunity to establish moral teaching for children and adolescents, we are best served to look to the principles that these founders used as they formed our nation. Our greatest opportunity to communicate who we are, where we stand, and how we operate will be in the success by which we can also apply these principles in our classrooms.

As one who serves children, whether in the classroom or the school office, one can rest in the knowledge that we've seriously considered the experience of those who created this nation. We share the same conceptual ideas as those first architects.

We cannot deny the simple understanding and articulations contained in the writings of those responding to the call to build a society exceptional to those that had existed to that point in history. Though some may be ashamed of or afraid of an accusation of national exceptionalism, we have to know that this nation was created as an exceptional model of democratic and free life pursuits.

Can we think as early Americans thought? Can we practice the elements of fair and collective good, without sacrificing those elements known by the moral nature of man as right and wrong? Can we know and teach that right and wrong is not subject to or victim of self-focused interpretation? Can we know there is agreement, within the heart, of those best things that will guide action and not violate the very things honored and acknowledged by the founding fathers?

We are encouraged that we can. The founding fathers adhered to agreements based on nondebatable understanding, knowing that those called to lead would create the artifacts necessary to express and honor a moral foundation. We reflect on these agreements and principles as well.

The following principles define our collective understanding and agreement. If we truly establish consistent and classical curriculum from generations past, we must continue in good and proven principles to move them forward for succeeding generations.

- We have a duty to elevate our classroom engagement with a strong and rigorous connection of moral education and sound academic pursuit.
- Following the pattern of good teaching and transferring wisdom and morality to generations of learners includes instilling in the young a profound regard for human life and a profound respect for the historical narrative of our nation.
- We have a duty to transform our learning environments, leveraging the best resources available, including the teacher and technology, to protect timeless and valued elements through the intelligent utilization and deployment of these current and emerging resources.
- A general and broad establishment of education for all citizens is an underlying insurance and a strong assurance of proper and organized transferring of knowledge, morality, and wisdom to generations.
- Moral exemplars are best defined by looking to educators who adhere to an external moral code and that moral code informs their practice and engagement with learners.
- The educator is endowed with belief systems that are present and effective that guide the individual to be ethical in the public administration of their duties, thereby adhering to professional mandates, yet impelled and influenced by these belief systems personally to engage with learners.
- The teaching of virtue, wisdom, and morality is not character education, nor is it self-esteem development, subject to the changing values and cultural preferences of man and society, but is instead a solid reliance on the undeniable inner knowledge of an absolute right and wrong.
- The family is the foundation for moral teaching, the rightful place for self-governance, and the central strength for any nation.
- Those who educate do not supersede, substitute, or subjugate the moral foundation of the family and will, by all means of practice,

provide supportive and strengthened pillars of reinforcement of family teaching.
- Those called to teach are first called to love children and adolescents in healthy and moral ways, providing guidance toward moral reasoning and wisdom.
- The primary duty of government is to protect the integrity of the family, minimize its intervention, and provide the structural vehicle to create free and lawful environments for peaceful citizenship.
- Our nation has an obligation to continue in its quest to be an example of what can be realized in a truly free and peaceful society.

Pedagogy has always informed the teacher as to practice in the classroom. Teachers have been the significant element of the education process and will continue being agents of learning experiences for students.

As our classrooms alternate dynamically between teacher-centered instruction and technology-supported environments, the role of a teacher will be no less significant. Whether the practice depends largely on the direct instruction of the teacher or the blending of technologically driven instruments, the educator continues to be the essential detail in the experience for the learner.

Those who serve families through teaching must commit to the idea that what we do with generations is most necessary for quality education, quality engagement with children and adolescents, and quality experiences between each other in the workplace. That quality is first defined by the foundation of moral education in the classroom, on the campus, and throughout this country. To believe less lowers our expectation for ourselves and others.

Morality cannot be legislated nor forced. Rather, it must be intrinsic and self-determined. Yet this self-determination must originate from and through personal belief systems. Those who are informed by personal and moral belief systems will best transfer those principles of moral dictates to generations of learners.

Though culture, perception, and social environments may change, transferring foundational moral principles to children ensures a sustainable and beneficial scope of good and virtuous living. How we treat our learners and how we interact with each other matters and our reliance on classical curriculum and moral teaching will continue what we committed to when we committed to this work.

SUMMARY

Some might wonder why it's important to weld the two parallels of intentional moral reasoning in education with current and emerging technology and teacher balances. As we have stated, the digital environment has changed, and will continue to change even more, the world of young learners.

And when these young learners become mature leaders, we have little capacity to know how consuming that technology may be. As this technology continues to expand and extend its reach into and through life, those adult generations will need what we can give them now. It's more than a diploma and a transcript.

A society wholly dependent on a vulnerable system must be able to flourish even if that system is suddenly taken from it. In other words, what happens if everything they depend on for their resources relies on a digital fluency and that connected technology system is suddenly disconnected?

And therein lies the purpose of why we need the forged-togetherness of both parallels.

The academic parallel is necessary because it prepares those generations for the world characterized and controlled by technology.

The moral reasoning parallel is necessary because it prepares them for the world when the system goes down.

Our learners depend on us. We must leverage all that we have to give them their best opportunity to thrive in a world demanding fluency in digital environments. But someone could pull the plug one day. Transferring wisdom and morality lifts those generations to greater heights to know how to thrive in that world as well.

To be good and do good, to be responsible for the good of others. To be noble and virtuous. To know that there is an absolute right and wrong while no one is absolutely right nor is everyone absolutely wrong. To look to their moral code and their moral reasoning.

And shepherd heart teachers are our best hope. May we encourage them, support them, and empower them to transfer that wisdom every day.

ABOUT THE AUTHOR

Dr. Alan Wimberley has worked with students since the late 1970s. Serving as the chief education architect for one of the largest nonprofit public charter systems nationally, a professor and doctoral chair for two universities, along with writing and speaking on genuine transformation in learning environments, he spends his time investing in current generations of educators to articulate, implement, and design learning systems in classrooms and on campuses. His previous book, *Reshaping the Paradigms of Teaching and Learning: What Happens Today Is Education's Future*, addresses the need to transform education nationally. An engaging and passionate speaker, his encouraging and motivating style connects with those who create good changes for learners every day. Most of his work, whether on a stage or around a table, benefits from his tremendous respect for those who teach, his rich experience of working with students and educators for years, and his motivating and dynamic style of teaching, training, and speaking. Having seen the changes in education for decades, he has proven to be one who can project where we are going and provide an architect's vision to get there. He works with districts, charters, and private academies to create relationships that transform from teaching systems to learning systems. Those interested in contacting Dr. Wimberley for speaking engagements, training opportunities, or engaging partnerships related to transforming education can contact him at (214) 418-1893 or by email at alanwimberley@gmail.com.

www.ingramcontent.com/pod-product-compliance
Lightning Source LLC
Chambersburg PA
CBHW030142240426
43672CB00005B/237